Architecture of the Old South

LOUISIANA

Architecture of the Old South
LOUISIANA

MILLS LANE

Special Photography by VAN JONES MARTIN

Editorial Assistance by JONATHAN FRICKER and ANN M. MASSON

Drawings by GENE CARPENTER

A BEEHIVE PRESS BOOK

Abbeville Press · Publishers · New York

Frontispiece: Parlange, New Roads, Louisiana, c. 1800

This book was conceived, edited, and designed by The Beehive Press of Savannah, Georgia.

Library of Congress Cataloging-in-Publication Data

Lane, Mills.
    Architecture of the Old South, Louisiana / Mills Lane : special photography by Van Jones Martin ; editorial assistance by Jonathan Fricker and Ann M. Masson ; drawings by Gene Carpenter.
        p.   cm.
    "A Beehive Press book."
    Includes bibliographical references (p.   ) and index.
    ISBN 1-55859-022-6
    1. Architecture, Colonial—Louisiana.   2. Architecture, Modern—19th century—Louisiana.   3. Architecture—Louisiana.   I. Martin, Van Jones.   II. Fricker, Jonathan.   III. Masson, Ann M.   IV. Carpenter, Gene. V. Title.
NA730.L8L36   1990
720'.9763—dc20   90-788
                                                          CIP

Unless otherwise credited, all photographs are by Van Jones Martin and all drawings are by Gene Carpenter.

Contents

LOUISIANA

0 10 20 30 40 50

This volume continues a series of books about the historic buildings of the Old South. Each volume illustrates and describes the important and beautiful buildings—restored, unrestored, demolished, and sometimes designs that were never executed—of one or two states, arranged in a sensible chronological and stylistic order and set in a brief cultural and social background. This sixth volume of the series is devoted to Louisiana, the French colony that became the most "foreign" of all Southern states. For valuable details on the area in the colonial period, the author is especially indebted to Samuel Wilson, Jr., the scholar-architect who has spent a lifetime studying the historic buildings of Louisiana and who shared his information with extraordinary generosity.

There have been many books about American architecture in general, but these surveys too often illustrate the same famous buildings, select didactic examples, and impose an artificial, if grand, orderliness on the subject. There have been few recent serious studies about the historic buildings of individual states. Many people know the most famous buildings of Louisiana—the Ursuline Convent, the Cabildo, Presbytère, and Cathedral in New Orleans, and the monumental columned houses along the Mississippi—or have at least heard ghost stories about the great lost buildings—the St. Charles Hotel, with its 185-foot-high dome, and Belle Grove, a gigantic Romantic villa, long a ruin, that burned many years ago. But even experts are unfamiliar with the contribution of French *émigrés* in the early 19th century, especially the brilliant J.N.B. dePouilly, or confuse the careers of the Irish-born James Gallier, Sr., and his son, James, Jr. Simply but significantly, the accumulation of many small bits and pieces of scholarly knowledge, with drawings and photographs, gives us the first comprehensive survey of Louisiana's historic architecture and shows the significance of succeeding generations of patrons, builders, and architects in a new light.

Buildings are three-dimensional history books that reflect the comings and goings, successes and failures of real people. Though Louisiana was never a very important French colony, the culture, language, and law of France prevailed in Louisiana long after the end of the colonial period. French-born builders and architects made unsurpassed contributions to the former colony till the Civil War. Outside the areas of French settlement, however, a different architectural tradition evolved in northern and eastern Louisiana, brought by settlers from the Eastern states. We devote an entire chapter to a close look at the Louisiana plantation house and the two separate traditions—French and English—that created the form.

The Civil War marks the triumph of industrialization in America, homogenizing the nation's cultural life and beginning the end of regionalism

Foreword

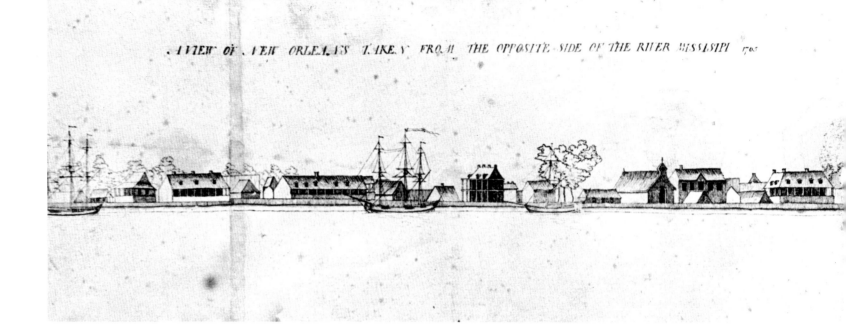

A VIEW OF NEW ORLEANS TAKEN FROM THE OPPOSITE SIDE OF THE RIVER MISSISIPI 1765

UNDER ☆ MY ☆ WINGS ☆ ☆ ☆ EVERY ☆ THING ☆ PROSPERS

Views of New Orleans: Top, anonymous drawing, 1765; bottom, left, painting by
John Boqueta deWoiseri, 1803; bottom, right, lithograph by J. W. Hill and Smith,
1852. *Louisiana State Museum, Chicago Historical Society, Private Collection*

in our country's architecture. Despite the name of this series, *Architecture of the Old South*, we have found that buildings throughout America were probably more alike than they were different. The great architectural styles—Adamesque Federal, the Greek Revival, the Gothic Revival—were all international movements. Professional architects from England and New York and Philadelphia introduced the Greek Revival to Louisiana. Most of the great buildings of the South were designed by professionals from outside the region or copied from builders' pattern books. The young and gifted James Gallier, Sr., and James Dakin, who had worked for Ithiel Town and Alexander Jackson Davis, came to the burgeoning port of New Orleans in the 1830's and produced buildings in the style of New York City. Cast iron and granite from Massachusetts, Cincinnati, and New York were often shipped to New Orleans. It seems evident that much of what some experts have described as Southern architecture is an accident of geography and exists mostly in the preconceptions of the beholder.

Nevertheless, the most "Southern" buildings of the Old South are also found in Louisiana, which endures the hottest, longest, and most humid summers in the region. Here wide porches and galleries, long windows, open stairways and halls, and raised basements were necessary accommodations to the severe climate. Somewhere in east-central Alabama there is an imaginary border that divides the older states of the upper and coastal South, with their more moderate climate and conservative building traditions, from the newer states of the lower South, with their harsher climate and freewheeling spirit. The origin of the traditional Louisiana house—with its raised basement and surrounding galleries—may never be completely clarified, but it either evolved in Louisiana in the mid-18th century or was brought to Louisiana from the Caribbean in the third quarter of the 18th century.

Indeed, upon a close look at the architecture of one state, the forces of localism seem, paradoxically, to be stronger than regionalism. Isolation from the southeastern colonies and different cultural origins gave Louisiana life and architecture a distinctiveness that has not yet been altogether lost. As we have already mentioned, even within Louisiana, settlers from North Carolina, South Carolina, and Georgia brought their own traditions that remained separate from the dominant French culture.

We have seen in previous volumes how Virginia had been the largest, richest, and most populous English colony in the South, with early architecture of unsurpassed richness and variety. South Carolina was also a well-established and prosperous colony with important buildings. But both Virginia and South Carolina began to suffer a relative decline in growth and quality of architecture by the late 1820's, when people were moving from the old, exhausted tobacco and cotton lands of the upper and coastal South to the fertile new lands of the Mississippi River Valley. North Carolina was also an early colony, but, with treacherous coasts, poor harbors, and shallow rivers, it was slow to develop. Georgia was the last and poorest colony, and less than a handful of pre-Revolutionary buildings has survived there. Georgia enjoyed its greatest prosperity during the heyday of the Greek Revival. Mississippi and Alabama, the two states carved from the historic Mississippi Territory, were settled principally after the 1830's and produced a surprising variety and quality of buildings in the relatively brief period before the Civil War.

Now that our exploration of the South has traveled all the way from Virginia to Louisiana, we begin to appreciate the relationship between the history and buildings of the old, well-established coastal states, Virginia, Maryland, the Carolinas, and the rougher frontier states, Georgia, Alabama, Mississippi, Tennessee, Kentucky, and Louisiana. Louisiana, established in the early 18th century and nurtured for nearly a century by French and Spanish culture, had so separate an identity that Louisianians of the early 19th century viewed Americans as "foreigners." This volume tells the stimulating story of Louisiana's distinct culture, carried from France by way of the Caribbean, challenged by a different culture, English in origin, that was brought by settlers from the Atlantic coast.

In our three final volumes, we will learn more about the great variety of buildings in Maryland, Tennessee, and Kentucky and then survey at last the history and architecture of the Old South in general.

I. *The Colony*

PLAN et ELEVATION de la CASERME des MENUISIERS

PLAN et ELEVATION de L' HOPITAL

French explorers first ventured to the lower Mississippi Valley during the 1680's, searching for new lands, trade, and military advantage over their Spanish and English rivals in the Old Southwest. In 1699, the first permanent French settlement on the Gulf of Mexico was established at Biloxi Bay in what is now Mississippi. In 1702 the capital and center of French activity was moved to the Mobile River in present-day Alabama. Two years later, there were 195 colonists in the French settlements, which were still concentrated in the area east of the Mississippi River. Not until 1715 was the first permanent settlement in present-day Louisiana established at Natchitoches on the Red River.

After the end of the War of Spanish Succession in 1713 and the death of Louis XIV two years later, French Louisiana was reorganized. New proprietors, the French West India Company, received a concession to develop the languishing colony. Eight hundred colonists were dispatched from France to populate Louisiana, and a new town was to be established as a trading center on the Mississippi River. In the spring of 1718 a clearing was made for this new town, New Orleans, on the left bank of the river, one hundred miles above its mouth, where an advantageous curve of the Mississippi offered a good harbor.

The first military engineer from France, Pierre Leblond de la Tour, a veteran of campaigns in Portugal, Spain, and Italy, reached Biloxi, Mississippi, in December, 1720. These engineers were professionally trained soldiers who were responsible for making maps, planning defenses and roads, and supervising the construction of buildings. Leblond was accompanied by three draftsmen and a group of workers. Many of the handsome drawings signed by the chief engineers for submission to the authorities in France were often actually drawn by skilled assistants like Bernard deVerges, Leonard Callot, Joseph Chauvin deLery, Franquet de-Chaville, and Valentin Alexandre Devin. In March, 1721, one of Leblond's assistants, Adrien dePauger, came to survey the new town of New Orleans and found "only a few huts among the bushes and trees."[1] The

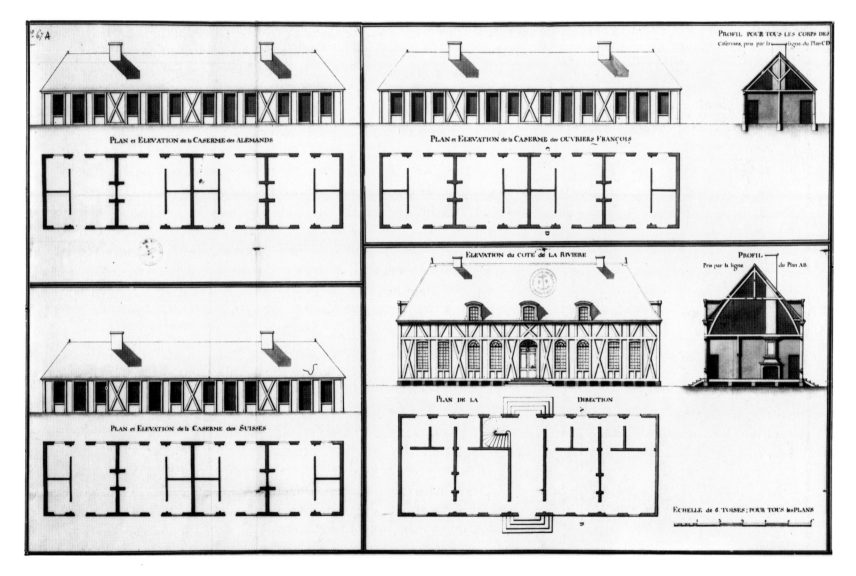

Plans, sections, and elevations of early public buildings at New Orleans, signed by Leblond de la Tour, January, 1723. This page: barracks for the Germans, barracks for the French workmen, barracks for the Swiss, and house for the manager of the colony. Opposite page: barracks for the carpenters and the hospital. *Archives de France*

most famous of these often obscure artists was Alexandre deBatz, who produced fascinating drawings of Indians and their villages in the 1730's. After twenty years spent working on public and private buildings for the French in the Mississippi Valley, deBatz died in 1759, while supervising the construction of forts in Arkansas and Illinois.

Pierre de Charlevois, a French-born Jesuit priest from Quebec who was holding church services in a tent, reported, in January, 1722, that New Orleans was then a village of "a hundred huts, placed in no very good order, a large warehouse built of timber, two or three houses which would be no ornament to a village in France [and] one-half of a sorry warehouse."[2] Later that same year New Orleans was made the capital of Louisiana and the first major buildings of the town were constructed: a headquarters, barracks for workers and soldiers, a warehouse for equipment and supplies, and a hospital. The hospital was fifty feet long and twenty feet wide and contained twenty-nine beds. In the absence of brick for foundations, the hospital was "built of wood . . . only planks on sills," with a shingle roof and exterior walls sheathed with wide horizontal boards, laid flush.[3] This hospital was completed in late 1722 under the supervision of Adrien dePauger. The official drawing, presented to the authorities in France to record completion of construction, was signed by Pierre Leblond de la Tour in January, 1723.

The timber-frame construction of the hospital and other early buildings illustrated in Leblond's handsome drawing recalls the 300-year-old farmhouses that visitors can still see scattered across the Normandy countryside—and also across much of northern Europe and England. Large timbers for the walls were shaped into long rectangles. It might take thirty great timbers, each fifteen by twelve inches thick, to assemble a small four-room, two-story house. The heavy timbers of the frame were fitted together with mortise-and-tenon joints and held in place with wooden pegs, a technique that would be used till the mid-19th century, when lightweight, machine-milled lumber and cheap, factory-stamped nails became available. Each timber was fitted together to form a skeletal frame and roof so carefully carved and joined that they became a work of art, something like the hull of a ship turned upside down. In the absence of bricks for foundations in Louisiana, the cypress frames of these first buildings rested directly on the ground.

In October, 1723, Leblond died and Adrien dePauger was appointed chief colonial engineer. He had been an engineering officer at Dieppe on the northern coast of France before coming to Louisiana in 1720. Pauger began work on a new warehouse, a powder magazine, a wing for the hospital, and a village church. The first colonists and soldiers had wor-

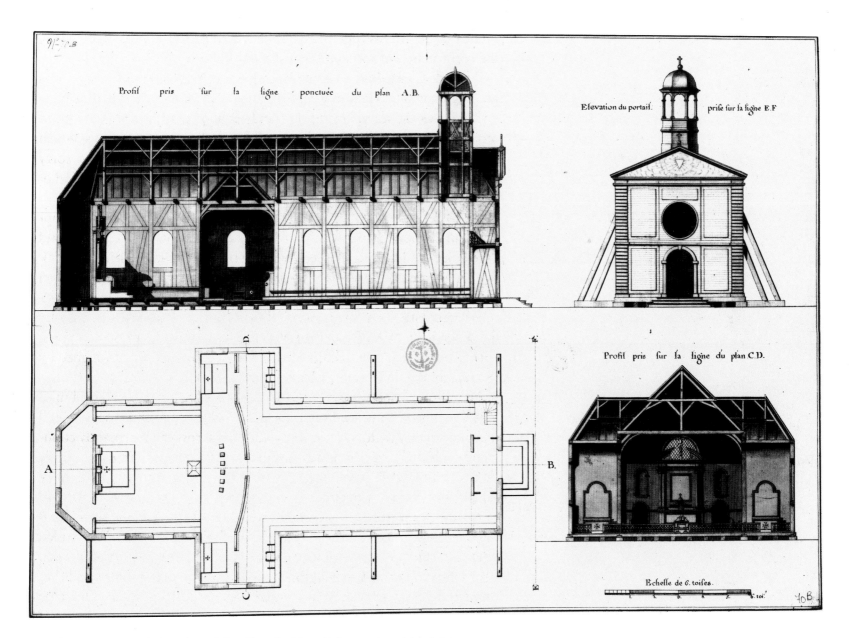

Profil pris sur la ligne ponctuée du plan A.B.

Elevation du portail. prise sur la ligne E.F

Profil pris sur la ligne du plan C.D.

Echelle de 6. toises.

Plan, section, and elevation of the Church, New Orleans, signed by Adrien dePauger, May, 1724. *Archives de France*

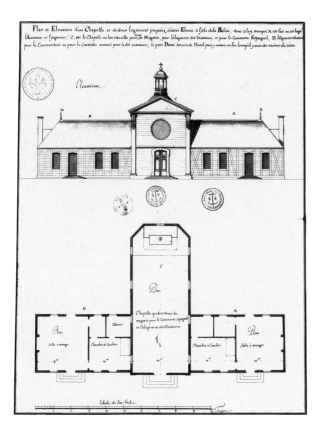

Plan and elevation of a chapel and two lodgings to be built at The Balise, c. 1723. *Archives de France*

shipped in makeshift churches—a tent, a decaying barracks, and a tavern. Pauger completed drawings for the church about February, 1724, when he asked the authorities in France to send religious statues and a stone tabernacle, "because if it were of wood, the many rats that there are here would entirely gnaw it away."[4] Bricks were still unavailable when Pauger began his design, so the architect planned to rest the cypress frame of the church, 112 feet long by thirty-two feet wide, directly on the ground, and he designed curious side buttresses to brace the building against hurricanes like one that had devastated the village in September, 1722. The church at New Orleans was similar to one Pauger had designed in 1723 at The Balise (in French, "the beacon"), a military garrison on an island at the mouth of the Mississippi.

Work on the new church at New Orleans proceeded with difficulty. In April, 1724, Pauger appealed to the authorities to raise workmen's wages to dissuade them from quitting—and especially the wages of the carpenter Pinault "to prevent him from being the leader to the other workmen."[5] Father Raphael, one of the Capuchin monks who were so eager for completion of the new church, complained that Pauger was making frequent changes to his plans and lacked the necessary skills for the work ("We have a carpenter here who could direct it better and at less expense than he does").[6] In June, 1725, a newly established brickyard on Bayou St. John began to produce bricks, though they were soft and porous, and Pauger decided to add brick foundations to the church and strengthen its walls by filling the spaces between the joists and braces of the timber frame with bricks, thus eliminating the need for side buttresses.

The church was still incomplete when Pauger died in June, 1726. His successor, Ignace François Broutin, born in northern France about 1690, had come to Louisiana in 1720 and been occupied erecting fortifications at Natchez. Broutin served as chief colonial engineer between 1726 and 1751, except for a brief period in 1729–31. In May, 1727, Broutin ordered glass for the church windows—and also "a glazier *or two*, in case one should die," and three good diamonds for cutting the glass.[7] The church was dedicated in December, 1727, but was never embellished with the pedimented reredos and Ionic columns shown in Pauger's elegant drawing of the interior. In 1731 the interior was still unplastered, and, because glass had not yet arrived from France, the window frames were "fitted only with cloth which is all tattered."[8] The altar was an old Spanish one, captured by the French at Pensacola in 1719. Like other early buildings, the exterior of the church was sheathed with boards. Abandoned for a few years in the late 1760's, the church, and the town hall, guard house, and parsonage that flanked it, burned in 1788.

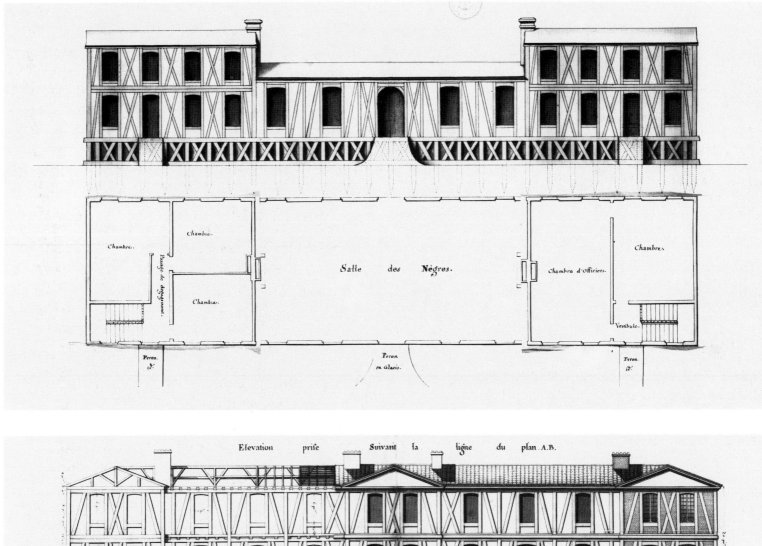

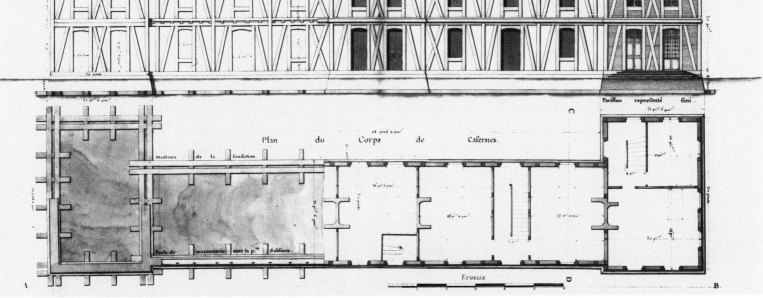

Top: Elevation and plan of a building to be built on the banks of the Mississippi at New Orleans, 1729. Bottom: Elevation and plan of one of two barracks to be built at The Balise, 1731. *Archives de France*

FAÇADE et ELEVATION du Bâtiment neuf Ruë du Maine Construit en l'année 1730. Fait et dessiné à la N.lle Orleans le 14. Decembre 1731.

Echelle de Trois Toises.

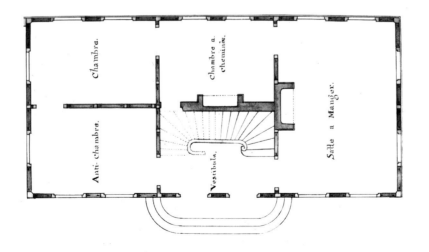

Elevation and plan of a house on the Rue du Maine, New Orleans, signed by Alexandre deBatz, December, 1731. *Archives de France*

After completing the church, one of Broutin's first projects was to build a convent for the Ursuline nuns who had come from Rouen to New Orleans in 1727 to run a hospital, orphanage, and school. In January, 1728, Marie-Madeleine Hachard, one of the nuns, reported: "They are working hard on our house. . . . The engineer came to show us the plan."[9] Workmen were scarce, as was the supply of roof tiles from local furnaces, and construction advanced slowly. By March, 1729, Michael Seringue, who had completed work on the church, began delivering lumber, window frames, door and other joiner's work to the site of the new convent.[10] Further progress was delayed in November, 1729, when a violent uprising of Indians at Natchez provoked so much alarm in New Orleans that laborers stopped work at the convent and began building a moat around the town. Broutin was sent to fortify Natchez against another attack.

In Broutin's absence, Pierre Baron, a naturalist with more enthusiasm for design than knowledge of building, insinuated himself with Governor Etienne dePerier and began acting as colonial engineer in Broutin's place. In August, 1730, Broutin complained to the authorities about modifications that Baron had made to the Convent: "I had made a plan of it, and it has been almost entirely changed without the least thing having been said to me about it. I will confess, gentlemen, that all this has not failed to disgust me greatly, considering all the pains that I took! . . . As far as the buildings that he is having built are concerned, I think that his draftsman, who is capable, has a greater part in them than he has."[11] That draftsman was probably the talented Alexandre deBatz.

The builder of the Convent was Claude Dubreuil. Born at Dijon about 1690, he came to Biloxi in 1718 and prospered as an indigo planter and manufacturer of brick. With the workers and capital to undertake public works, Dubreuil soon established himself as a builder. With Franquet deChaville, he built the first levee at New Orleans in 1724 to protect the low-lying and fever-infested town from flooding.[12] The nuns finally moved into the new convent in July, 1734. The lower floor contained a chapel, two parlors, a room for the mother superior, a dining hall for boarders, a kitchen, a small office, the nuns' refectory, a common room, and hospital office. The second floor contained fifteen chambers, a dormitory, and two rooms for the sick. The third floor was for the use of boarders and orphans. Baron's most unfortunate change to Broutin's plan was to leave the exterior walls unprotected by weatherboarding or stucco; in the rainy climate, the timber frame and its porous and soft brick in-fill deteriorated rapidly.

Limited supplies of materials were a nagging problem during the early years in Louisiana. The Church had been delayed by slow delivery of

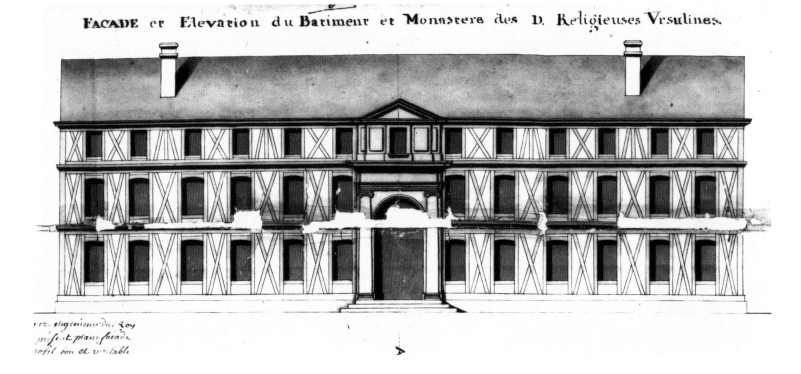

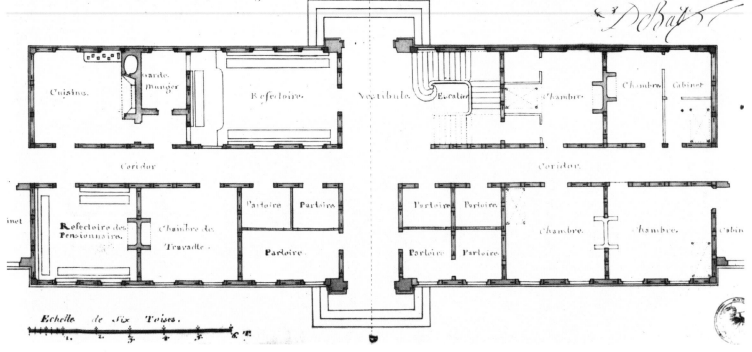

Elevation and plan of the Ursuline Convent, first design, signed by Ignace François Broutin and Alexandre deBatz, 1732. *Archives de France*

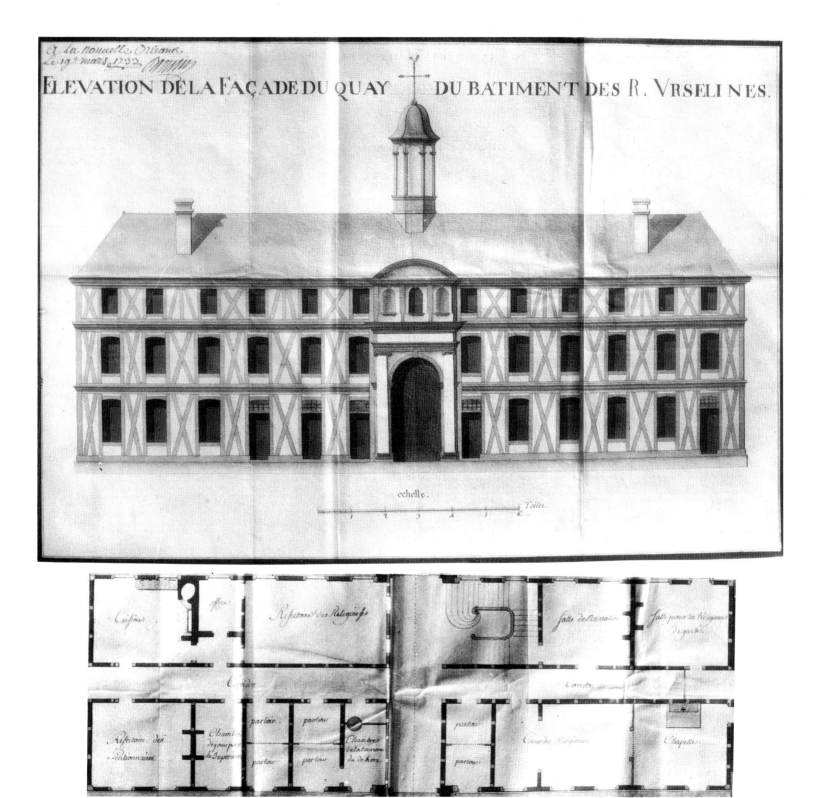

Elevation and plan of the Ursuline Convent, revised design, signed by Ignace François Broutin, March, 1733. *Archives de France*

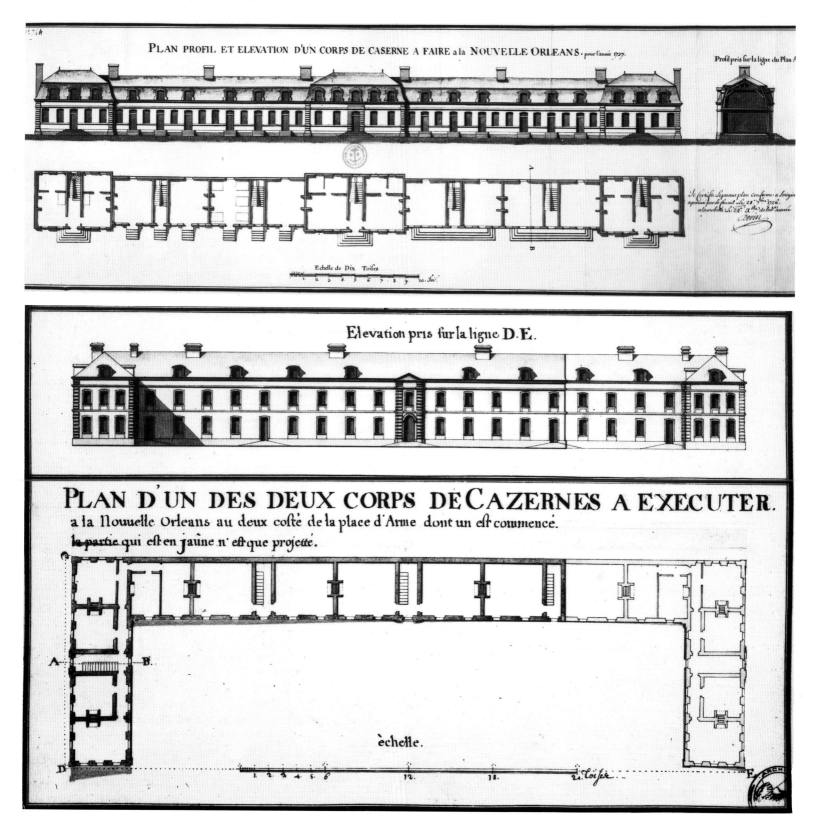

PLAN PROFIL. ET ELEVATION D'UN CORPS DE CASERNE A FAIRE a la NOUVELLE ORLEANS. pour l'année 1727.

Profil pris sur la ligne du Plan A

Echelle de Dix Toises

Elevation pris sur la ligne D.E.

PLAN D'UN DES DEUX CORPS DE CAZERNES A EXECUTER.

a la Nouuelle Orleans au deux costé de la place d'Arme dont un est commencé.
la partie qui est en jaune n'est que projetté.

echelle.

Top: Plan, section, and elevation for barracks to be built at New Orleans, signed by Valentin Alexandre Devin, 1727. Bottom: Elevation and plan of one of two barracks to be built at New Orleans on two sides of the public square, signed by Ignace François Broutin, 1734. *Archives de France*

lumber, and the Convent had been delayed by a limited supply of clay tiles. In September, 1723, a carpenter named Adrien Gilbert built a model of a sawmill to be operated by hand or horse power, promising to produce 150 planks a day. The indefatigable Gilbert also presented models for a river dredge and a rice mill, and in 1725 he attempted to refloat a wrecked vessel in the river.[13] The first sawmill was built in 1728 and began operation in 1729.[14]

In 1725 a German colonist was granted extra rations, the use of four blacks for two years, and financial aid to help him produce bricks for the colony.[15] The first brickyard was established outside New Orleans on Bayou St. John in September, 1726, employing several white artisans and fourteen black workers.[16] During its first twenty-five months of operation, the yard produced 400,000 bricks. In 1728 two masons sent from France complained that they were receiving only one pot of brandy per month instead of the two pots that they had been promised as an incentive to come to Louisiana.[17] About 1727 a second brickyard was established by the Jesuits outside New Orleans. By August, 1730, there were some forty workers in this brickyard. The first brick building, a hospital wing added to the Convent to replace the old frame Hospital destroyed in 1732, was completed in 1733. In September, 1752, Honoré Michel de la Rouvellière could report from New Orleans: "In the three years I have been here about forty fine houses of brick have been built."[18]

Meanwhile, Baron returned to France in 1733 and Broutin again became chief engineer of the colony. In 1734, after several years of indecision, the authorities determined to build a new Barracks at New Orleans. After considering several designs intended to be built on the outskirts of the town, they decided to build two structures on opposite sides of the square in the center of the town. Broutin's dignified design, with its pediment, quoins, stringcourses, and mansard roof, is notable for its many academic details. The plan, however, with its lack of cross-ventilation, was less successful. Broutin's obvious failure to adapt to the torrid climate is not surprising when we note that the design was copied from Plate 29 of Bernard Belidor's *La Sciènce des Ingenieurs,* a manual on military construction published at Paris in 1729. The Barracks were built in 1734–39 by Claude Dubreuil. They were demolished in 1759.

When Broutin submitted drawings for a Doctor's House in 1737, the authorities approved its refined design with the hope that it would improve the taste of the town, saying: "We have considered that it would be proper to give it an agreeable form so the citizens, who up till now have been living in only sorts of cabins, can copy it when they can afford substantial buildings."[19] Most of the 1,100 people of New Orleans in 1740

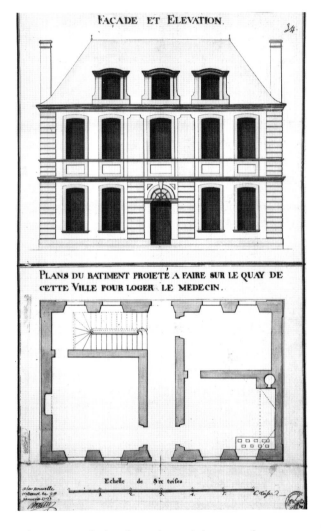

Elevation and plan for a doctor's house to be built on the quay at New Orleans, signed by Ignace François Broutin, 1737. *Archives de France*

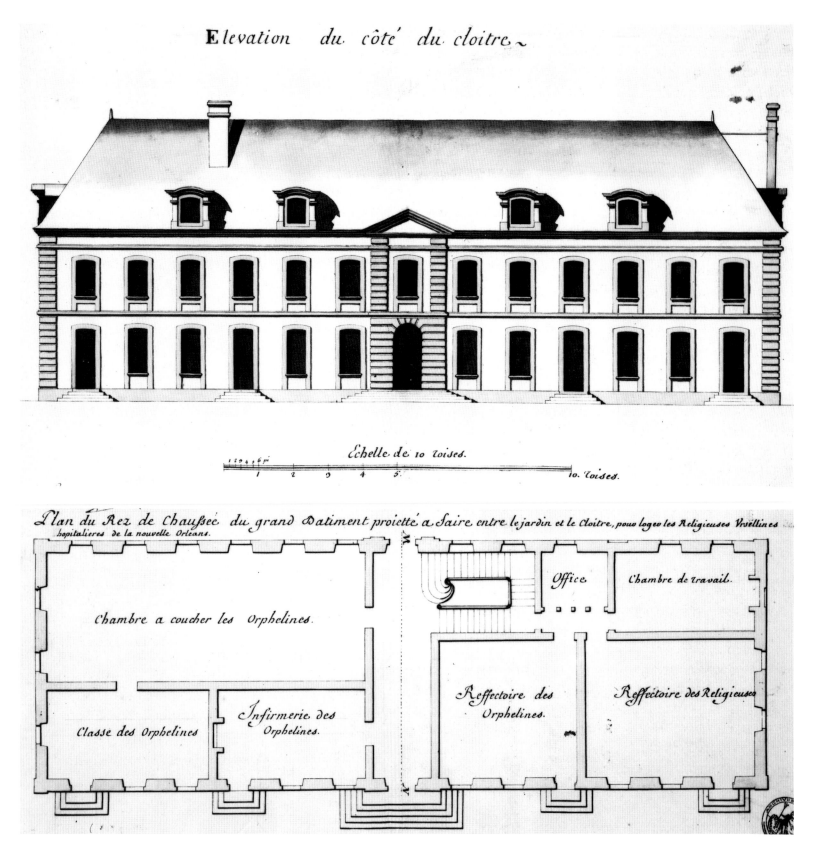

Elevation and plan of the second Ursuline Convent, New Orleans, signed by Ignace
François Broutin, 1745. *Archives de France*

lived in simple huts (*cabanes*) constructed with vertical cypress posts buried in the ground (*poteaux-en-terre*), the spaces between the posts filled with a mixture of mud, moss, and twigs (*bousillage*). Inch-thick sticks were inserted between the studs rather like a ladder with the rungs about six inches apart. Moss or sometimes animal hair was mixed with mud and shaped by hand into blocks, which were then packed tightly between the sticks and allowed to dry. The surface on each side of the wall was smoothed and covered with a coat of fresh mud or plaster. The floors were hardpacked earth, and roofs were bark or, like early French forts along the Gulf, "palms whose leaves are flat and arranged like a fan."[20] Huts of this general type are documented as far away as 17th-century Virginia and early 18th-century Georgia—and as late as the 19th century in Louisiana (see pages 61–62).

More substantial buildings were timber-framed, but their sills were placed directly on the ground (*poteaux-sur-solle*) and not on brick foundations until the brickyard opened in 1726. Until then, houses were expected to last only three to six years. In 1730 Marie-Madeleine Hachard, one of the Ursuline nuns, wrote that some houses were "well built, with upright joists, filled with mortar between the interstices, and the exterior whitewashed with lime . . . the interior . . . wainscotted."[21] Sister Marie wrote that, though she lived in "the most beautiful house" in New Orleans, two stories high with a mansard roof and large windows, there was "no glass but the sashes are hung with fine cloth which gives as much light as glass."[22] In November, 1727, another colonist complained that "Every six months we have to change the linen cloths that are put on the windows because they rot."[23]

By 1745 the convent of 1734 was beginning to collapse. Construction had been delayed, and the timber frame, long unroofed and exposed to rain, was rotting. In addition, Pierre Baron had neglected to protect the exterior walls with weatherboarding, which further accelerated the decay. Broutin produced the design of a new Convent in 1745, and construction was undertaken in 1748–53 by Claude Dubreuil. Parts of the old building, including the massive stair of cypress and wrought iron, were salvaged for use in the new edifice. The Ursuline nuns occupied the Convent until 1824. Later it was used as a bishopric, schoolhouse, state capitol, and seminary. Now used as the archives of the archdiocese, the Convent is the oldest surviving building in New Orleans—and also the oldest in the Mississippi Valley—since no others date before the 1780's.

After Broutin died in 1751, Bernard deVerges succeeded him as chief colonial engineer. Having come to Louisiana as a draftsman in 1720, he remained chief engineer until his death in 1768. Louisiana was a weak

Colonial office, New Orleans, built by Bernard deVerges, 1763, detail from a map of the city by Jacques Tanesse, 1817. *Louisiana State Museum*

and undeveloped collection of thinly populated settlements along the bayous and waterways between Mobile and Natchitoches, and in New Orleans, with seven thousand colonists, slightly fewer than the number thirty years earlier. The French and Indian War disrupted public works in Louisiana and resulted in the dismemberment of the French empire in America, when the British seized Canada and France ceded New Orleans and Louisiana west of the Mississippi to Spain, and the rest of Louisiana to Britain, in 1762–63. The Spanish governor, with an ineffectual force of ninety soldiers, did not reach New Orleans until 1766 and then was threatened with a revolt by the French inhabitants of the city. Though the colony flourished during the Spanish regime, French culture, French law, and the French language prevailed, just as the German colonists who came to the *bayou des allemands* in the 1720's had been absorbed into the dominant French civilization. The colonial office erected at New Orleans by deVerges for the French in 1763 continued to serve as the seat of successive governments—Spanish, American, and the state of Louisiana—until it burned in 1828.

In 1769, there were 1,865 whites, 1,225 blacks, and 468 houses in New Orleans. In the late 1760's, Philip Pittman, a young British lieutenant sent from New York to survey French forts along the Gulf coast, wrote that most of the houses of New Orleans were "built of one floor, raised about eight feet from the ground, with large galleries round them and the cellars under the floors level with the ground . . . with timber frames filled up with brick." [24] The oldest house now standing in New Orleans is one built about 1788 for Manuel de Lanzos, a Spaniard, by Robert Jones, an American. Like the buildings described by Pittman and similar buildings pictured by the artist John Boqueta deWoiseri in 1803, this house features a raised brick basement, walls of thick cypress timbers and *bousillage*, a front gallery, small chambers (*cabinets*) at each end of the rear gallery, and long casement windows in place of sashes or hinged doors. De Lanzos's house, popularly known as Madame John's Legacy, at 632 Dumaine Street, has been restored by the State of Louisiana.

A disastrous fire in 1788 destroyed some nine hundred houses in New Orleans, and another in 1794 destroyed two hundred more. In the aftermath of this alarming devastation, the Spanish authorities prescribed new building regulations for New Orleans. Instead of rangey wooden cottages, with open galleries and steep, cypress-shingled roofs, the 1795 regulations required that all new houses within the central fortified area be built of brick, or timber frames filled with brick and coated with cement or lime one inch thick, and covered with a flat roof of tiles, square brick, or other fireproof material. [25] In 1801, John Pintard, a merchant

"Madame John's Legacy," built for Manuel de Lanzos, 632 Dumaine Street, New Orleans, c. 1788.

from New York, observed: "The roofs in general are quite flat & paved with square tiles. . . . All the Houses are plaistered . . . ballustrades 'round the roofs . . . with their columns, urns & balls."[26] In the following year, John Sibley, a physician from Massachusetts, noted: "The Greatest Number of the Houses . . . are flat Roofed. They first lay on Strong Beams, a little sloping thin planks, then Plaister or lime, earth & Tar, then Brick Tile lay'd in Lime, over all & Rough coat of Tar Lime & Oyster Shells . . . a Balustrade 'round ornamented with Urns, Balls, &c. and the tops of the Houses are as their Back yards, Women wash, iron, sit to Work & the Men walk on them."[27] In 1808, Christian Schultz, land speculator from New York, wrote of New Orleans: "The houses of the principal streets nearest the river are built of brick covered with slate, tile, or fire-proof construction." Schultz noted that the city then had 12,000 people and 1,100 houses.[28] In 1819, the English-born architect Benjamin Latrobe wrote: "The houses are, with hardly a dozen exceptions among many hundreds, one-story . . . covered with tiles," and he noted stuccoed façades painted yellow or white, long casement windows, and wide eaves that overhung the sidewalks.

The decayed church of 1724, and the guard house and parsonage flanking it on the town square, had burned in the fire of 1788. The following year, the design for a new church was provided by Gilbert Guillemard (1746–1808), the most interesting architectural personality of the Spanish period. Born in France, well trained in mathematics and military design, Guillemard had been an engineer in the service of Spain at Baton Rouge, Mobile, and Pensacola before coming to New Orleans about 1770. The new church was consecrated as St. Louis Cathedral in 1794. It was described by Dr. John Sibley in 1802 as "a large Brick Building with Two Steeples, no Galaries, lofty Pitched & Arch's supported by five Doric pillars on each Side done with White Stocko, about the pulpit on each Side are a Variety of Images, Pictures, &c. which look Grand & Elegant—the floor is paved with Smooth tile. . . . On Each Side are Long Seats Raised a little."[29] A clock tower was added to the Cathedral in 1820 by Benjamin Latrobe. The present building dates almost entirely from 1849–52, when it was rebuilt in enlarged form by J. N. B. dePouilly.

Guillemard also designed the Presbytère that was to be built on the upriver side of the Cathedral. The walls had been raised only one story high by 1798, when the private sponsor of the building, Andres Almonaster y Roxas, died. Construction was interrupted and a temporary roof was put on the incomplete shell. It remained in place until 1813 when the builders Claude Gurlie and Joseph Guillot added a second story. The Presbytère was enlarged in 1840 by Benjamin Buisson and again in 1847

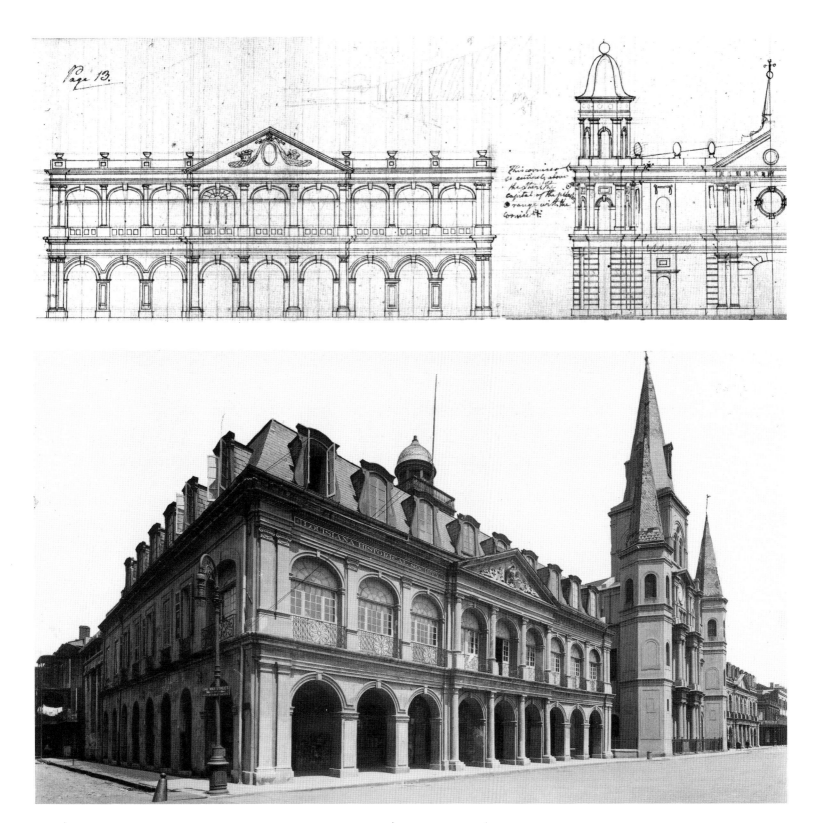

The Cabildo, Cathedral, and Presbytère, New Orleans. Top: drawing by Benjamin
H. Latrobe shows the Cabildo and Cathedral, 1789–94, as they appeared about
1820. *Maryland Historical Society*. Bottom: Photograph of the 1920's shows the
Cabildo with the mansard roof added by Louis Surgi in 1847 and the new Cathedral built by J.N.B. dePouilly in 1849. *Historic New Orleans Collection*

when a mansard roof was added by the city surveyor Louis Surgi. Though intended to be a parsonage for the Cathedral, the Presbytère was rented for use as a store, apartments, and a courthouse. The building now belongs to the Louisiana State Museum.

Gilbert Guillemard also designed the Cabildo, the town hall, to be built on the downriver side of the Cathedral where a one-story frame building of 1769 had stood before the fire of 1788. The new Cabildo incorporated surviving walls of the old French guardhouse that had also stood on part of the site before the fire. The American eagle and trophies of military victory, inspired by the Battle of New Orleans in 1815, were added to the building's pediment in 1821. The mansard roof was added to the Cabildo by Louis Surgi in 1847. In 1792 Guillemard provided the design for five forts that the Spanish authorities planned to build in place of the old French palisade around New Orleans. Between 1795 and 1800 Guillemard devised bridges, walls, a fish market, and additions to the Royal Jail.

Another French-born architect of the Spanish period was Barthélémy Lafon (1769–1820).[30] Born in the southern province of Languedoc, Lafon reached Louisiana by 1787 and prospered as a surveyor, engineer, land speculator, and city alderman. He repaired the levees along the Mississippi River, operated an iron foundry, and owned many architectural books. In January, 1797, Lafon petitioned the city authorities for land on which to build an immense bathhouse. Designed in late 1796, Lafon's bathhouse was to have been a two-story stuccoed brick building, with a rusticated first story and a monumental Ionic portico surmounted by a balustrade and urns. Efforts to raise money and obtain land must have failed, for the magnificent bathhouse was never built.

Lafon probably designed the lavish mansion of Samuel Moore, a Massachusetts-born merchant, that was built two streets away from the levee about 1799–1800. John Pintard exclaimed in 1801: "I know of no front either in N York or Philadelphia to a private house that can compare with it!"[31] Dr. Sibley wrote of Moore's mansion in 1802: "The walls are Brick, the front highly ornamented, the passages are floored with Marble & the Back Salon [has] Marble Chimney Pieces, [there are] 2 flights of Mahogany Stairs of four Stories each, the hand Rail round the Stair Walls [rises] without a Break, the Roof of the Front is Slated . . . a Balustrade all round. . . . The Carved work of the Chimney Pieces & Arching of the Windows and Sides is very Rich & Handsome, the Cornishing Rich and Bold."[32] Samuel Moore's mansion has been demolished, and there is no drawing or photograph of it.

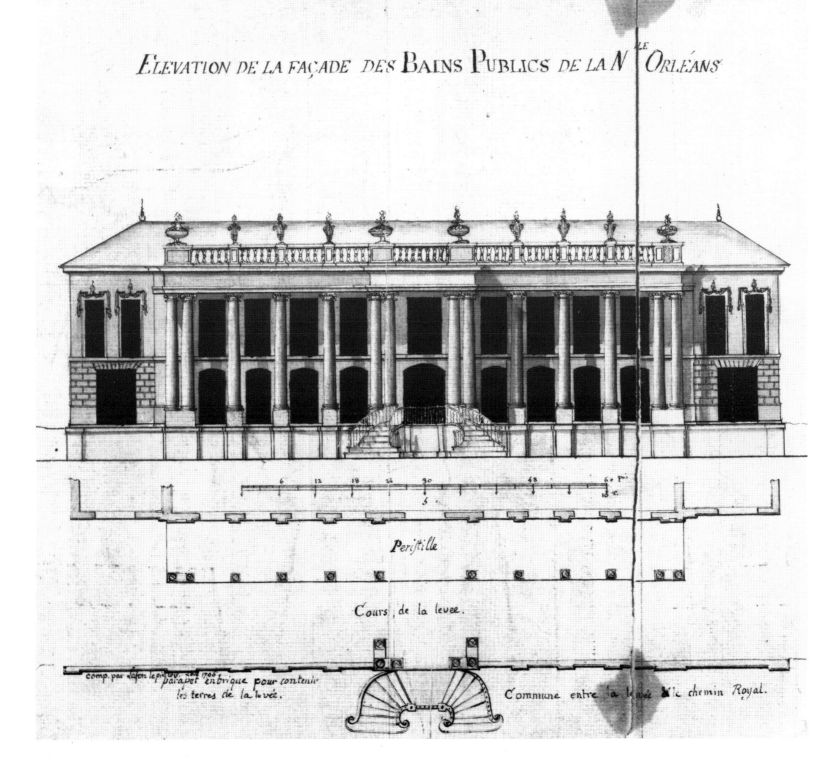

Public Baths, New Orleans, design by Barthélémy Lafon, 1797. *Louisiana State Museum*

II. *The Federal Era*

When France sold Louisiana to the United States in 1803, the population of present-day Louisiana, excluding Indians, was some 50,000 people, of whom 32,000 lived along the banks of the Mississippi River and 9,000 lived in the port of New Orleans. In the 1790's, the Mississippi had become the vital waterway for settlers in Ohio, Tennessee, and Kentucky. The cotton gin had been devised in Georgia in 1793, and a process for granulating sugar was developed by a Louisiana planter, Etienne de Boré, in 1794. As the older states of the Eastern seaboard began to suffer from crowding and depleted soil, settlers from Virginia and the Carolinas migrated to Georgia, Alabama, and the Old Southwest. By 1810, the population of New Orleans had already reached 24,000. In January, 1812, the first steamboat came down the Mississippi to New Orleans from Pittsburgh. In April, 1812, Louisiana was admitted to the Union as a state, just six weeks before war was declared against Britain. During the last year of the War of 1812, New Orleans was the major objective of a British invasion of the Mississippi Valley. In January, 1815, an army of 5,000 Americans under Andrew Jackson withstood an assault by some 9,000 British regulars. The great battle for New Orleans was international recognition of the importance of the river and the port.

Throughout the early 19th century, but especially during the early years of the territorial period, French designers and builders continued to make unsurpassed contributions to Louisiana architecture. French culture was reinforced by an influx of some 10,000 refugees who fled to Louisiana after slave uprisings on the French island of Santo Domingo in the 1790's.[1] In France, Louisiana—remote and alluring—became the background for literary works like Chateaubriand's *Atala* of 1801, the love story of two savages in Louisiana, and for Romantic paintings inspired by them.

Gilbert Guillemard, the French engineer who had been in the service of Spain since the 1770's, continued active in New Orleans until his death in 1808. Barthélémy Lafon, another French engineer, worked in New Orleans from 1787. In 1805 he produced an important early map of Louisiana. Two years later he issued the first New Orleans city directory. In 1808 Lafon designed a city meat market. During the War of 1812 he served as a military engineer with the Americans. In 1816, faced with financial difficulties, Lafon was forced to sell his possessions, including a treasured library of 450 volumes. Lafon died of yellow fever in 1820.

Jean Hyacinthe Laclotte (1766–c. 1829) came to New Orleans from France in 1804 at the age of thirty-nine.[2] Descended from a family of builders in Bordeaux, he had practiced architecture for many years in France. His passport stated that Laclotte was going to Louisiana "to practice his art."[3] Laclotte must have been eager to begin buildings for the burgeoning port, for, upon his arrival, he announced plans for a courthouse, exchange, market, college, and public gardens. In July, 1805, he proposed erecting a new theater on the site of the old Spanish custom house. This theater was to be 222 feet long, 138 feet wide, surrounded by an arcaded terrace, with a Corinthian portico and roof balustrade surmounted by allegorical statues. The interior would have had a semicircular auditorium seventy-one feet long and sixty feet wide, with two ranges of boxes and a proscenium arch embellished with stars for the states and an eagle representing the new nation.[4]

This theater was to have been built by Louis Tabary, a theatrical impresario who declared bankruptcy before construction could commence. However, Laclotte's proposals of 1805 were probably incorporated into the design of the Orleans Theater, which was begun in October, 1806, burned in 1816, and rebuilt in 1817–19. In 1807 Laclotte designed a turret and circular stair for the Cabildo to provide access to the roof for fire watchmen. Because of its cost, the design was never executed. In February, 1807, Laclotte offered his "services for the building of houses in town and country . . . with elevations and perspective views in a precise and agreeable manner."[5] Laclotte spent 1808–10 in Mexico.

Meanwhile, another French-born architect, Arsène Lacarrière Latour (c. 1770–1839) came to New Orleans about 1808 by way of Santo Domingo. Latour provided designs for a public market in 1808 and for another new theater, the St. Philip Street Theater, in 1810. In Laclotte's absence, Latour supervised construction of the Orleans Theater. Upon Laclotte's return to New Orleans in 1810, Latour and Laclotte, both living in the house of the widow of Gilbert Guillemard at the corner of Royal and Orleans streets, became partners offering "to undertake the building of all public and private edifices, to direct all kinds of building on adopted plans, to draw up estimates" and "plans for the laying out of houses . . . for Gardens, Parterres, decorations of apartments, drawings

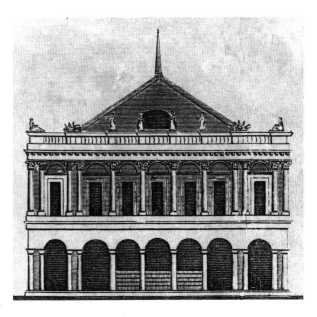

Orleans Theater, New Orleans, 1806, detail from a map of the city by Jacques Tanesse, 1817. *Louisiana State Museum*

St. Philip Street Theater, New Orleans, 1810, detail from a map of the city by Jacques Tanesse, 1817. *Louisiana State Museum*

Mariners Church, New Orleans, design by Joseph Pilié, c. 1827, redrawn from original in New Orleans Notarial Archives.

of fancy furniture."[6] Latour and Laclotte also opened a school to teach "drawing in its various branches . . . the designing and colouring of plans, levelling perspective, ornament, architecture in all its branches, the composition and distribution of plans, the details of carpenter's work, joinery, masonry, smith work, &c., &c., the distribution, ornamenting and furnishing of apartments in the newest taste, and according to the principles adopted in the Paris academy of fine arts, of which they are both pupils."[7] After only three years, this partnership was dissolved in March, 1813. In July, Laclotte, then living in a house next door to the Orleans Theater, offered to "execute plans and decorations of all types and . . . take pupils in drawing and architecture."[8] In 1815, Laclotte and Latour served as military engineers under Andrew Jackson. After a sojourn in Philadelphia, Laclotte returned to France in 1821.

In the late 18th and early 19th centuries, before architecture developed into a specialized profession, artists often dashed off designs for buildings and architects also worked as engineers. Joseph Pilié (c. 1789–1846), a refugee who came to Louisiana after the slave revolts on the Caribbean island of Santo Domingo, practiced as an architect, engineer, and artist. When he reached New Orleans in 1808, Pilié opened "a school of drawing in which he teaches Drawing, Portraits, Landscape, Artificial Flowers, as also Architecture and its principles, in the manner of copying, reducing and colouring Plans."[9] For a time Pilié was associated with Barthélémy Lafon.[10] In 1816–17 Pilié was working as a painter of theatrical scenery. About 1827 he designed the Mariners Church, a graceful neoclassical building with a commanding stair, entablature, console-like gable, and a cupola, but the church was never completed. Eight years after construction had commenced, the traveler Joseph Holt Ingraham described the abandoned church as "a huge, dark colored, unshapely pile of brick . . . never finished and seldom occupied except by itinerant showmen with their wonders."[11] Working as city surveyor for many years, Pilié designed a parish prison, a long, three-story brick building with an arcaded ground story and rooftop balustrade. Construction was begun on Orleans Street in 1833 by the builder Samuel Slack but was interrupted when the walls had reached the top of the first story. Construction was resumed by Edward Correjolles and John Chaigneau. After revisions to the original design had been made by J. Voilquin, the prison was finally completed under the direction of A. Bourgerol and C. Crozet in 1838. The prison has been demolished.

Another French architect of the period was Benjamin Buisson (1793–1874), an engineer, surveyor, and amateur astronomer who came to New Orleans in 1817, built a custom house in 1820, and became state architect in the early 1830's. Allou d'Hémécourt, a French architect, civil engineer, and surveyor who had some association with Joseph Pilié, reached New Orleans in late 1827, when he announced that he had "just arrived" from France and would open a school of architecture, mathematics, and drawing and was ready to undertake architectural work.[12] In 1849, d'Hémécourt submitted a design for the remodeling of St. Louis Cathedral, a project that would be undertaken by another French architect, J. N. B. dePouilly.

The forgotten career of Jacques Nicholas Bussière dePouilly (1804–1875) is another example of persistent French influence in Louisiana and one of the most exciting rediscoveries of Southern architectural history.[13] DePouilly came to New Orleans about 1833, endowed with brilliant artistic gifts and a highly professional knowledge of world architecture. Though no evidence has been found that dePouilly was formally enrolled at the famed École des Beaux Arts in Paris, he may have studied in one of the many ateliers, or studios, that were associated with the École. Founded in 1819, from the ruins of the old Royal Academy, the École des Beaux Arts offered a rigorous and disciplined program of apprenticeship and study of Classical architecture culminating in competition for further study in Athens and Rome.

It was in recognition of dePouilly's outstanding knowledge and skill that he was selected in an 1835 competition to design one of the most important buildings of New Orleans, the St. Louis Hotel and City Exchange, a vast structure containing a hotel, merchant exchange, assembly rooms, public baths, a bank, and shops.[14] Occupying half of an entire block on St. Louis Street, the Hotel was actually three buildings—exchange, hotel, and shops—built in stages so that Hewlitt's Exchange, located at one corner of the site, could operate without interruption. The long façade was unified by a series of first-story arches, whose repetitive regularity was a typical feature of French Classicism. Similar façades were erected along the Rue de Rivoli in Paris, which Napoleon ordered built in 1811. The St. Louis Hotel was completed in 1838.

DePouilly also designed an entirely new street, Exchange Place, which began at Canal Street, the principal commercial thoroughfare, and led to the front door of the Hotel on St. Louis Street. Reflecting the best of late-18th- and early-19th-century town planning in France, dePouilly intended that the five blocks of Exchange Place would be lined with three-story shops and offices of unified design, providing a ceremonial approach to the Hotel. This visionary plan was never fully implemented, and the most complete block of Exchange Place was demolished in 1910 to make way for a new courthouse.

St. Louis Cathedral, design by Allou d'Hémécourt, redrawn from original in New Orleans Public Library.

Exchange Place, a 19th-century view. *New Orleans Notarial Archives*

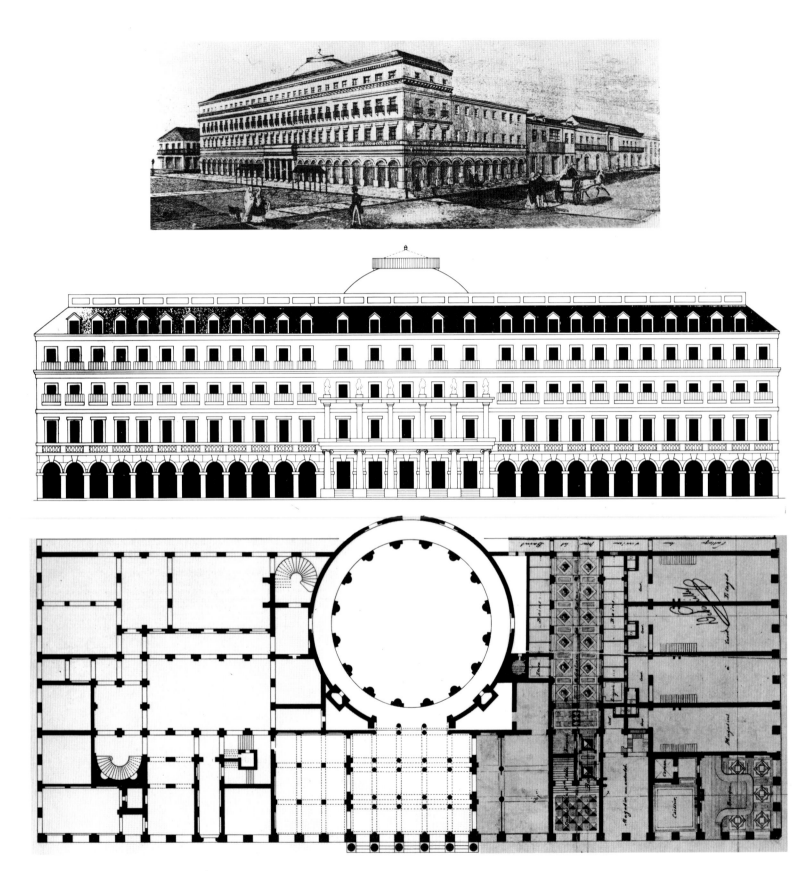

St. Louis Hotel and City Exchange, New Orleans, 1835–38, an early 19th-century
engraving, a conjectural restoration of the elevation, and dePouilly's original plan,
the left portion of which has been redrawn from a damaged manuscript, the right
portion being dePouilly's drawing. *Print from Historic New Orleans Collection,
manuscript drawing from New Orleans Notarial Archives*

After making his way along Exchange Place, the 19th-century visitor could sweep beneath the Hotel's shallow portico, formed by six Doric columns surmounted by statues, across a vestibule 127 feet long and forty feet wide, into a central rotunda. The rotunda was reserved for business gatherings, deal-making, and auctions during the early afternoon and for parties at night. It was sixty-six feet wide and rose to a dome eighty-six feet high. Sixteen Corinthian columns, forty feet high, were stuccoed and marbleized, with bases of iron and capitals of black cypress. The walls of the rotunda were embellished with "Arabesques and Fresco paintings . . . emblematic of the various commercial cities in Europe and America." [15] Lighted by a fourteen-foot-wide oculus, the dome was an ingenious construction of hollow clay pots reinforced with sixteen wrought-iron ribs. The interior of the dome was embellished with sixteen medallion portraits of American heroes, including Washington, Franklin, Jackson, Decatur, Columbus, Clinton, Jefferson, Monroe, Hancock, Madison, Vespucci, Hamilton, Lafayette, and William Henry Harrison. The rotunda was flanked by a barroom and a reading room. A separate entrance on St. Louis Street led to assembly rooms on the second story. [16] Another entrance on Royal Street led directly into the Hotel. When the St. Louis Hotel burned in 1840, it was immediately rebuilt, but the second building was demolished in 1906.

DePouilly also provided the design for the Citizens Bank, located behind the Hotel on Toulouse Street. Built for the New Orleans Improvement Company, which had financed the Hotel, the Bank was connected to the exchange room of the Hotel by a small rear passage. In March, 1837, dePouilly journeyed to the Northern states to obtain granite for the Bank's magnificent Corinthian portico. The architect's drawing, dated April, 1836, suggests the splendor of the interior, as well as the intricate construction of the Bank's vaulted ceiling. [17] The Citizens Bank was completed in 1838 and demolished about 1910.

During the 1830's, J. N. B. dePouilly worked with his brother, Joseph Isidore dePouilly (1810–1866), in an office on Exchange Place. They also operated a mill that produced lumber and plaster. Two projects from their years of collaboration are recorded in building contracts or sketches: the residence and pharmacy of Joseph Dufilho, 514 Chartres Street, opposite the St. Louis Hotel, in 1837, and a three-story house for Marianne Olivier, at 828 Toulouse Street, featuring a central doorway flanked by arched passageways, leading in the "French" manner to a rear courtyard, in 1839. [18]

During the 1840's, J. N. B. dePouilly worked with Ernest Goudchaux, a builder born in France about 1793. Their projects included rebuilding

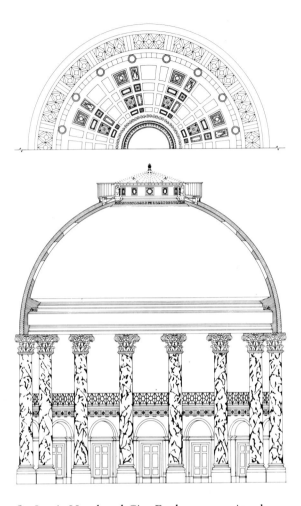

St. Louis Hotel and City Exchange, sectional view of the rotunda, based on dePouilly's damaged manuscript in the New Orleans Notarial Archives.

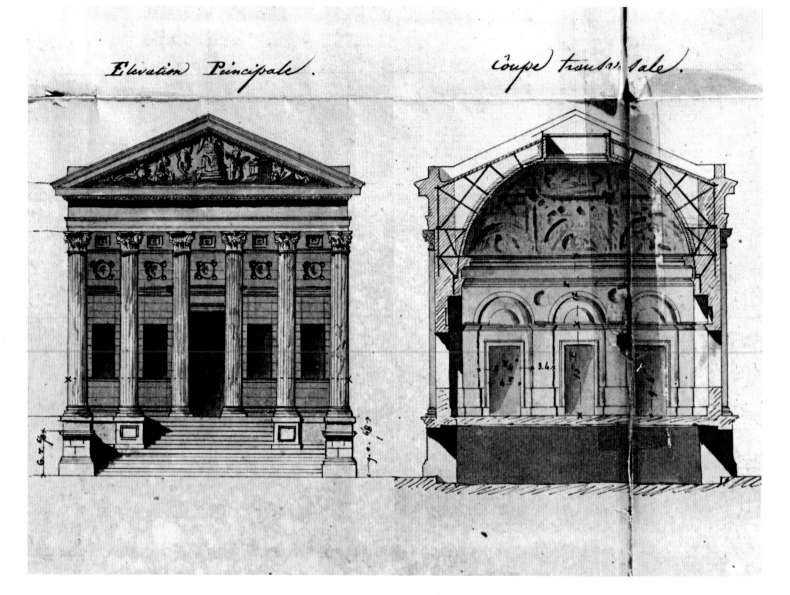

Elevation Principale.   *Coupe transversale.*

This page and opposite: Citizens Bank, Toulouse Street, New Orleans, 1836–37, dePouilly's elevation, sectional view of interior and plan, with an early view of the exterior before its demolition about 1910. *Drawings from New Orleans Notarial Archives, photograph from Louisiana State University Library, Baton Rouge*

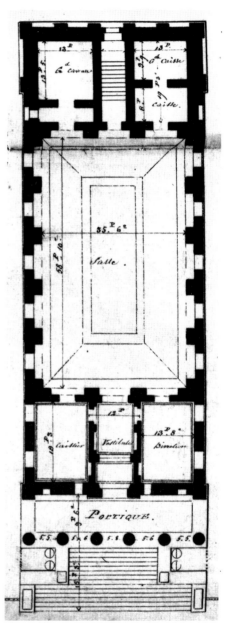

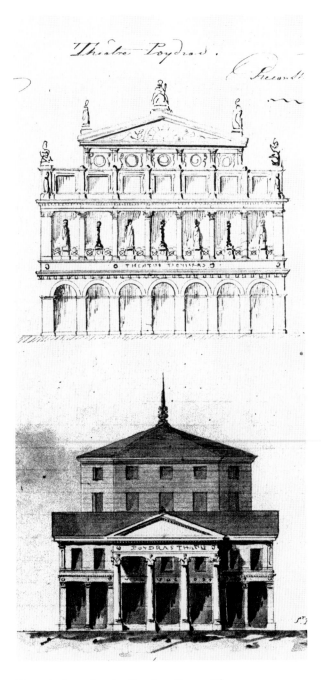

Two designs for the Poydras Street Theater,
New Orleans, by J.N.B. dePouilly, 1840–42.
Historic New Orleans Collection

the Poydras Street Theater for the theatrical managers Ludlow and Smith in 1840–42; the St. Augustine Church on the Bayou Road, 1842; a house for Edward Bertus at 826 St. Louis Street, 1842; a house for Eugénie deSafsize on St. Louis Street in 1842; a house for Augustine Avart at 632 St. Peter Street, 1842; repairs to the Orleans Theater in 1845; a two-story house on Thalia Street for Francisco dePaula Para, 1846; a store for Alexander Graihle on Poydras Street, 1849; and five three-story brick stores on Poydras Street for Zenon Trudeau in 1849.[19]

In 1849, dePouilly began work on a project so ambitious that it probably destroyed his career as a designer and builder. In February, 1849, dePouilly delivered plans and specifications for rebuilding St. Louis Cathedral on the *place d'armes*.[20] He had experimented with several other ideas, but his final neoclassical design featured three tiers of superimposed Doric, Ionic, and Corinthian columns, surmounted by statues of saints and an intricate Gothic steeple of cast iron and wood. Work was begun by the builder John Kirwan, but in February, 1850, dePouilly's new tower collapsed, bringing down part of the roof and walls. DePouilly and Kirwan were dismissed, and rebuilding of the Cathedral was completed by Samuel Stewart at the end of 1851. Only the foundations of the main tower, the lower parts of the façade, and corner towers from the old building were salvaged for use in the new Cathedral. The Cathedral's collapse was followed by another embarrassment for dePouilly in 1854, when the gallery and second-tier boxes of the Orleans Theater, which he had redesigned and rebuilt in 1845, collapsed. Although the accident was probably caused by faulty cast iron, the architect's reputation was seriously tarnished. Henceforth important commissions eluded the talented dePouilly, and he was obliged to accept a subordinate position in the city surveyor's office.

The purchase of Louisiana by the United States in 1803 was followed by a flood of energetic and ambitious Americans from the North and East into the territory. By 1820, the population of New Orleans, doubling during the previous decade, reached 41,000. These newcomers brought with them the Adamesque Federal style from Atlantic ports that were closely linked to England by commerce and culture. Despite the young nation's protestations of independence, American builders continued the traditions of English architecture in the post-Revolutionary era. In the mid-18th century English builders copied the monumental forms of ancient public buildings as published in the works of the late-Renaissance architect Andrea Palladio and his English popularizers. Palladio used columns, pediments, and projecting pavilions to suggest the giant porticoes of ancient Roman temples. These monumental forms were

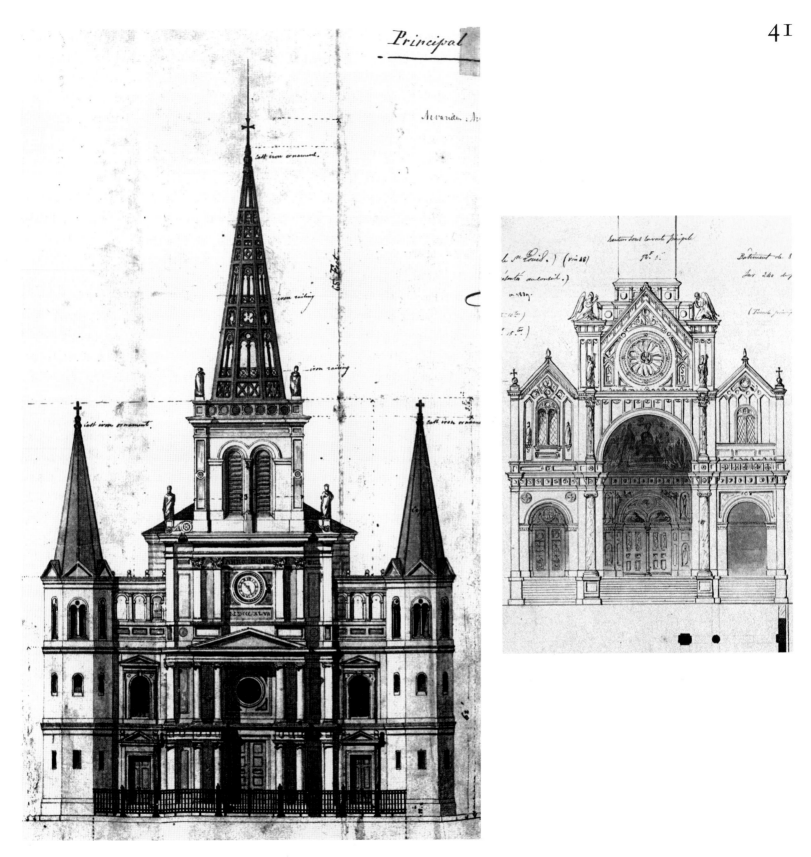

Design for rebuilding St. Louis Cathedral, New Orleans, by J.N.B. dePouilly, 1849, and an alternative Romanesque design by the same architect. *New Orleans Notarial Archives, Historic New Orleans Collection*

enriched in the last decades of the 18th century by an intricate delicacy that reflected a rediscovered knowledge of ancient domestic architecture, usually called the Adam style after Robert Adam, the Scottish-born architect who popularized it. Craftsmen from the Eastern cities brought with them to Louisiana knowledge of Roman porticoes, Tuscan columns, and Palladian windows, and also fanlights, cascading spiral stairs, and swirling patterns of surface decoration that is known in America as the Federal style.

One of the "American" newcomers to New Orleans was Benjamin Latrobe (1763–1820), a professionally trained architect from England. Latrobe, the son of an Irish-born Moravian minister and an American-born mother, was born in Yorkshire and studied engineering in London. When he sailed to America in 1796, he brought with him a firsthand knowledge of current English architectural fashions. With his professional training enhanced by amazing artistic gifts, Latrobe was by far the most talented architect in America in the early 19th century. He worked in Virginia for three years, 1796–99, and then moved to Philadelphia. Appointed surveyor of public buildings at Washington in 1803, Latrobe helped design and construct buildings of the new capital.

As early as 1806 Latrobe had been told about the burgeoning port of New Orleans by his friend and mentor Thomas Jefferson. Latrobe designed a Custom House to be built at New Orleans in 1807–09 by Robert Alexander (1781–1811), a Virginia-born carpenter who built the Washington Navy Yard that Latrobe had designed and who owned the house that Latrobe rented in Washington.[21] Bricks and marble for the Custom House were imported from Philadelphia, and carpenter's work was prefabricated at Washington. Because of weak foundations and soft bricks, the Custom House deteriorated rapidly and was replaced in 1820. Latrobe also designed a lighthouse to be built at the mouth of the Mississippi River, but its construction was delayed by the War of 1812.

Latrobe's career was as vertiginous as it was brilliant. Frustrated by professional opportunities that seemed too modest for his tremendous talents and burdened with an impatient and sometimes prickly personality, Latrobe moved frequently in search of work, living in Philadelphia until 1807, then in Washington, 1807–12, Pittsburgh, 1813–15, again in Washington, 1815–18, and Baltimore in 1818–19. In 1809 Latrobe conceived a plan to design, finance, build, and operate a waterworks at New Orleans. Water from the Mississippi would be pumped by a steam engine into six raised reservoirs and then fed by gravity throughout the low-lying town in five thousand feet of wooden pipes. In 1810 Latrobe

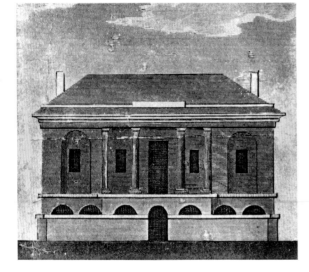

Custom House, New Orleans, by Benjamin H. Latrobe, 1807–09, detail from a map of New Orleans by Jacques Tanesse, 1817. *Louisiana State Museum*

designed the buildings for the waterworks and sent his son Henry to New Orleans to promote the project and begin construction.

Though described by his father as "a warm-hearted boy of eighteen" who got into trouble with cards and liquor, Henry Latrobe was already a professional architect who had studied with his father and Maximilian Godefroy in Baltimore.[22] In addition, with a French-sounding name and fluent knowledge of that language, Henry was well prepared to represent his father before the proud French authorities of New Orleans. While pleading for extensions of his father's contract with the city, Henry erected the engine house for the waterworks in 1811–12. The engine house was a small two-story octagonal brick building flanked by one-story wings, containing offices and living quarters for the engine keeper. Significantly, the engine house featured a one-story Doric portico, the first example of Greek architecture in the Old Southwest.

In 1813 Henry Latrobe was busy supervising 247 men who were constructing barracks for soldiers at Fort St. Leon, sixteen miles downriver from New Orleans. In 1814 Henry provided a design for Christ Church, an octagonal brick building with a cupola on Canal Street. The Church began to collapse in the mid-1830's and was replaced by a new building on the same site. During the Battle of New Orleans in 1815, Henry served as assistant engineer under Lacarrière Latour, with whom he had built a small, one-story tile-roofed house for Jean Baptiste Thierry at 721 Governor Nichols Street the previous year. In 1815–16 Henry built Charity Hospital on Canal Street, with third-story windows cleverly designed to appear to be extensions of the second-story windows. This building was converted into a state house in 1835 and demolished about 1850.

In 1816 Henry Latrobe designed and built Assembly Rooms beside the Orleans Theater for the theater's owner John Davis. Despite his English-sounding name, Davis was a French refugee from Santo Domingo. The theater and Assembly Rooms burned in September, 1816, and were immediately rebuilt. In 1816 Henry also erected a house for William Kenner, a Virginia-born commission merchant and sugar planter who was a vestryman of Christ Church. Instead of French-style casements, this house featured innovative sash windows "hung with weights in the American style."[23] In the busy year of 1816 Henry also designed a lighthouse, a circular tower eighty-one feet high surrounded by a colonnade of twenty Doric columns, probably based on his father's design of 1806. The lighthouse, built near the mouth of the Mississippi by Winslow Lewis from Boston, collapsed as it was nearing completion. Henry Latrobe died of yellow fever in September, 1817.

Engine House, New Orleans Waterworks, by Benjamin H. Latrobe, 1811–12, detail from a map of New Orleans by Jacques Tanesse, 1817. *Louisiana State Museum*

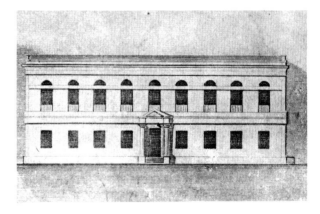

Charity Hospital, New Orleans, by Henry Latrobe, 1815–16, detail from a map of New Orleans by Jacques Tanesse, 1817. *Louisiana State Museum*

Louisiana State Bank, Royal Street, New Orleans, 1820–22. *Library of Congress*

Meanwhile, progress of the waterworks had been long delayed by technical difficulties, the war with England, and lack of money. But Benjamin Latrobe, reduced to bankruptcy in late 1817, continued to hope desperately that he might at last make in New Orleans the fortune that had so far eluded him elsewhere in America. In December, 1818, Latrobe, who had been trying without success to have a steam engine for the waterworks built in Pittsburgh, finally purchased an engine in Baltimore and sailed to New Orleans to complete the waterworks. In the spring, he designed a new clock tower, one hundred feet tall, for St. Louis Cathedral and devised improvements and a fountain for the public square in front of the Cathedral. In March, 1819, Latrobe designed a house for Vincent Nolte, an Italian-born banker, on the corner of Toulouse and Royal streets. Latrobe wrote his wife, who was still in Baltimore, with news of the commission for Nolte: "This business will help me on here and enable me to bring home some money, I *hope*."[24]

After returning to Baltimore in the fall to bring his wife to Louisiana, Latrobe was back in New Orleans by April, 1820. In the early summer, he designed the Louisiana State Bank on Royal Street.[25] A two-story brick building constructed with fire-resistant brick vaults instead of timber joists, the Bank contained a business hall and offices on the first story, paved with black and white marble, and living quarters for the cashier on the second story. The original roof was nearly flat but was later replaced with a tall hipped roof. Like the best of Latrobe's buildings in Philadelphia and Baltimore, the Louisiana State Bank featured bold geometry, facilitated by sophisticated engineering, expressed by springing vaults, shed of unnecessary ornament, reduced to thin, flat surfaces and finely chiseled decoration, flavored with Greek as well as Roman details.

In the late summer of 1820, as Latrobe was nearing completion of the long-nurtured waterworks and construction of the Louisiana State Bank, New Orleans was visited by yellow fever, an annual plague in the early 19th century. In August, Latrobe wrote to the Baltimore lawyer Robert Harper: "There is no denying the fact at present that yellow fever exists in the city. Of 30 Men in my employ, most of them drinking men, all but two have been sick, two have died *drunk*!"[26] In September, after a day of wading along the muddy banks of the Mississippi installing pipes for the waterworks, Latrobe himself caught the disease. Though cruelly "bled and blistered" in the custom of the era, Latrobe died, three years after the death of his son from the same sickness. The waterworks finally began operation in 1822, and the city continued to operate Latrobe's system until 1840.

Plan of Louisiana State Bank.

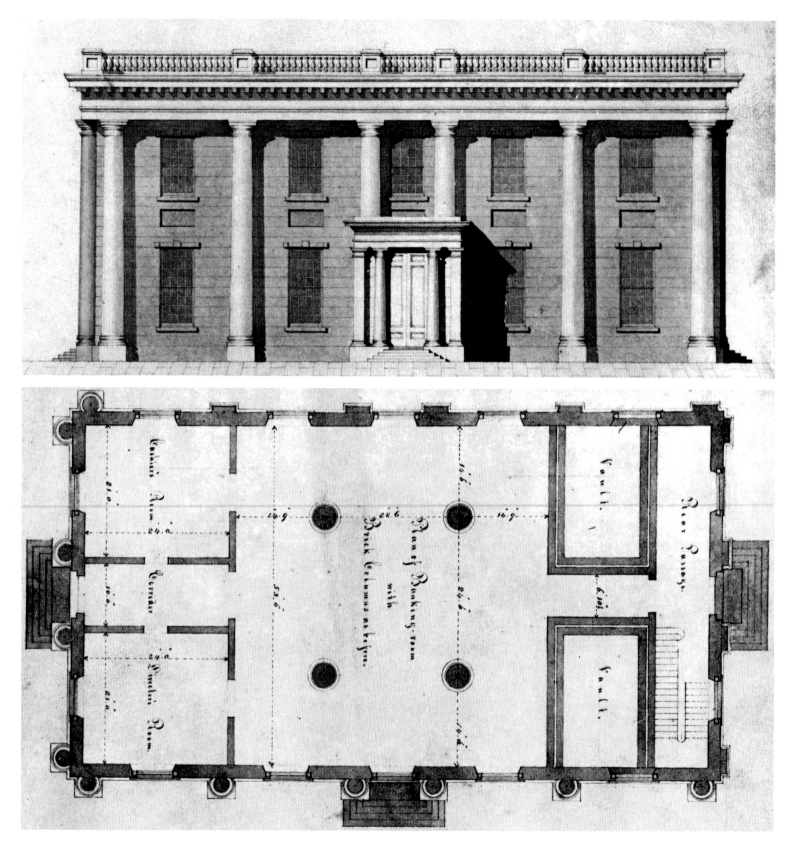

Bank of Louisiana, 334 Royal Street, New Orleans, 1826–27, drawings by James Gallier, Jr., c. 1861, showing the original plan but new one-story vestibule (not on the plan) and Doric capitals on the exterior. *Labrot Collection, Southeastern Architectural Archive, Tulane University Library, Gift of Sylvester Labrot*

The Louisiana State Bank was completed by carpenter Benjamin Fox in 1820–22. Fox had repaired Henry Latrobe's Christ Church in 1820 and built its rectory in 1825. In 1826–27, with Tobias Bickle (1785–1834) and Philip Hamblet (died 1831), Fox built the Bank of Louisiana at 334 Royal Street, diagonally across the street from the Louisiana State Bank. Damaged by fire in 1861, the Bank was refurbished by James Gallier, Jr., who added a new portico and substituted Doric for Ionic capitals on the engaged columns of the exterior. The Bank of Louisiana later served as a temporary state capitol in 1869–70 and as an auction house, concert hall, and city offices in later years. Benjamin Fox was contractor for the carpentry work at the United States Mint at New Orleans in 1835–38.

Before his death, Benjamin Latrobe had surveyed the burgeoning port of New Orleans and observed: "Americans are pouring in daily, not in families but in large bodies. . . . The leading Gentlemen, when not talking of tobacco or cotton, find it very amusing to abuse & ridicule French morals, French manners, & French houses. . . . The merchants from the old United States . . . having already begun to introduce the detestable, lopsided London house . . . [and] red brick fronts . . . I have no doubt but that the American style will ultimately be that of the whole city, especially as carpenters from the eastern border of the Union are the architects &, of course, work on in their old habits."[27] The scholar-architect Samuel Wilson, Jr., has located a striking example of changing architectural fashion in New Orleans. In 1825 Joseph LeCarpentier hired Thomas Rose and Alonzo West to build a house with many traditional French features, including a long front gallery that also served in place of an interior hall and interior stair. Construction was interrupted or never begun, for in 1826 LeCarpentier hired James Lambert to build a different house on the same site, this one an "American" house with a pedimented portico leading into an interior hall with a stair.

William Brand (1778–1849) came to the United States from Scotland in 1792 and made his way to New Orleans, probably by way of Virginia and Kentucky, about 1805. Brand was a mason who also operated a brickyard. He was contractor for the brickwork at the Orleans Theater in 1810 and for Davis's Assembly Rooms when they were rebuilt in 1817. In 1819 Brand built the First Presbyterian Church, the earliest Gothic building in New Orleans. In 1820 Brand repaired Christ Church, the octagonal brick structure designed by Henry Latrobe in 1814. Other projects included a brick house on Canal Street for Benjamin Denys in 1820, a brick building on Canal Street for Messrs. Phelps and Babcock in 1823, a house on Chartres Street for Nicholas Destrehan in 1825, five

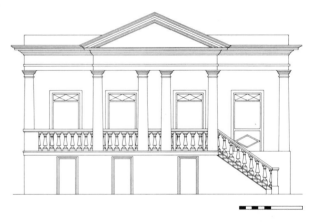

Joseph LeCarpentier House, New Orleans, the 1826 design for an "American" house redrawn from original in New Orleans Notarial Archives.

Samuel Hermann House, 820 St. Louis Street, New Orleans, 1831–32.

Parlor and dining room of Hermann House.

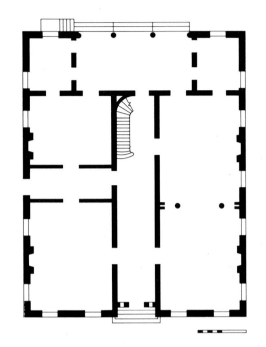

Plan of Hermann House.

Camp Street Theater, right, built for John Caldwell in 1822–23. The Arcade Baths, left, built for Caldwell in 1835–36 by James Gallier, Sr., and James Dakin. *Historic New Orleans Collection*

houses on Chartres Street for Joseph Soniat and a building on St. Louis Street for John LaPretre in 1827, and a building on Madison Street for Michel Nicaud in 1830. In February, 1831, Samuel Hermann, a German-born commission merchant, hired Brand to construct a house at 820 St. Louis Street. This was one of the earliest and most prominent "American" houses in the heart of the French district. The severity of its plain brick front, lacking the traditional gallery, was emphasized by painting the bricks bright red and penciling the mortar joints. An expansive fanlight entrance leads into a wide central hall. Hermann House, known as Hermann-Grima House, is open to the public. Brand continued active in the building business until the late 1830's, when he retired to Louisville, Kentucky.

In 1804 the old decaying wooden fortifications surrounding the French city had been demolished by citizens eager for firewood during an unusually cold winter. The proud French citizens of New Orleans must have viewed the Americans with mingled envy and distrust. As the city spread beyond its 18th-century boundaries, the Americans tended to congregate in a swampy area above Canal Street, an open space reserved for a canal that was never completed. In 1819, Latrobe noted: "The American suburb already exhibits the flat, dull, dingy character of Market Street in Philadelphia or [a] Baltimore street."[28] Oakley Hall, a newspaper scribbler from the East, later described the American quarter as "here a little of Boston, there a triffle of New York, and some of Philadelphia."[29]

Prominent among the "American" newcomers to New Orleans was the English-born actor and theatrical manager James Caldwell. Only twenty-seven when he reached New Orleans at the end of 1819, Caldwell was an indefatigable showman and promoter of himself and his projects for civic improvement. Caldwell became a city alderman and state legislator, organized a gas company that brought artificial illumination to New Orleans, and planned a 500-mile railroad between the port and Nashville. In 1822–23, Caldwell financed the Camp Street Theater. This was the first theater in the American quarter, isolated in the middle of muddy, mostly vacant land three blocks above Canal Street, but the Theater seated 1,100 spectators in grand style and was illuminated by the city's first gaslights.[30] The Camp Street Theater burned in 1842. Rebuilt as a dance hall, it was finally demolished in 1881.

Caldwell's greatest architectural project was the St. Charles Theater, built behind the Camp Street Theater on St. Charles Street in 1835. Caldwell also planned to construct an arcade of shops, a hotel, restaurant, bathhouse, and club rooms beside his two theaters.[31] The St. Charles Theater featured a Corinthian portico surmounted by statues of Apollo

St. Charles Theater, New Orleans, 1835, a 19th-century drawing. *Historic New Orleans Collection*

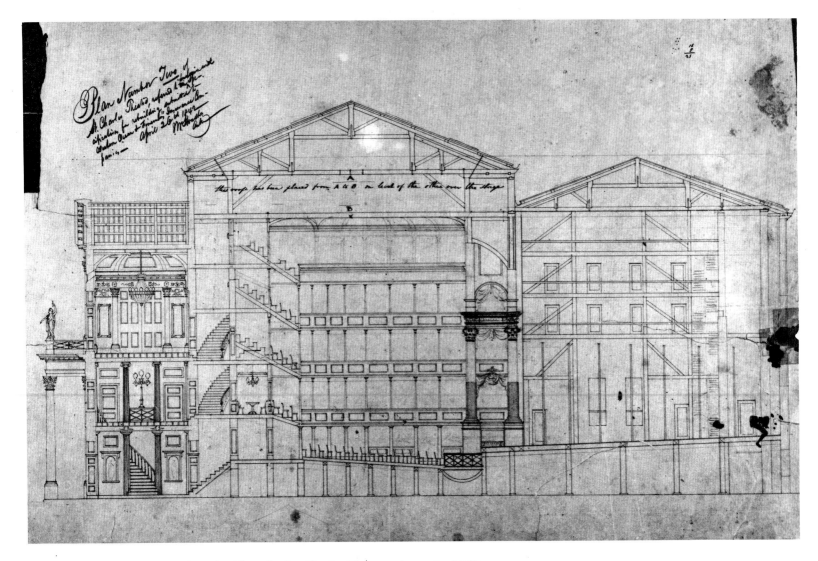

Sectional view of design for rebuilding the St. Charles Theater, drawn by William Houston, 1842. *Southeastern Architectural Archive, Tulane University*

and the muses. The auditorium contained four tiers of boxes and balconies.[32] After an 1842 fire, the Theater was rebuilt within its old walls.

The designer of the St. Charles Theater was Antonio Mondelli (1799–1864). Born in Italy, Mondelli reached New Orleans by 1821, when he offered his services as "Painter, Decorator, Gilder, Drawer and Glazier" and opened an art school in his house on the corner of Dumaine and Royal streets.[33] In 1824 Mondelli was painting scenery at the Camp Street Theater. He exhibited panoramic views of Paris and London, the white cliffs of Dover and the English Channel, and scenes of famous naval battles and Mt. Vesuvius erupting.[34] In 1826 Mondelli offered to teach the "Art of Painting, also Architectural Designing." In 1834 he advertised himself as a "house, sign and ornamental painter . . . glazing, paper hanging . . . imitations of every kind of marbles and woods, decorations in all its branches in oil and water colours."[35] Mondelli's diverse activities illustrate again how the profession of architecture in early America, still unspecialized and mostly self-taught, was practiced by carpenters, bricklayers, amateurs, and artists. For many years Mondelli worked as a builder with John Reynolds (1798–1858), who came to New Orleans from Philadelphia about 1820. In 1838 Mondelli and Reynolds submitted a design for a proposed United States Marine Hospital to be built near New Orleans. In 1847 they prepared plans for a proposed capitol to be built at Baton Rouge. In September, 1851, Mondelli was fined $20 for carrying a concealed revolver "and threatening to shoot somebody with it."[36]

In June, 1835, while the St. Charles Theater was under construction, the State of Louisiana hired the builder Edward Sewell to remodel the old Charity Hospital as a state house.[37] The design for a large rear wing, containing a hall for the state representatives, with sixteen fluted Corinthian columns, was provided by William Nichols, who was working as assistant state engineer under Benjamin Buisson. Nichols (1773–1853) was born at Bath and sailed from England to North Carolina in 1800. He worked in New Bern, Edenton, and Fayetteville for twenty years; appointed state architect of North Carolina in 1820, Nichols remodeled the state house at Raleigh in 1820–24. Nichols worked in Alabama as state architect between 1827 and 1833—designing a capitol, university, and Episcopal church at Tuscaloosa—and in Louisiana for two years before moving to Mississippi in 1835.

The burgeoning port of New Orleans was attracting ambitious and talented merchants and builders from New England and the Middle Atlantic states, who were rapidly changing the face of the city. Elsewhere in Louisiana, along quiet bayous and dirt roads, older traditions persisted in the areas of early settlement.

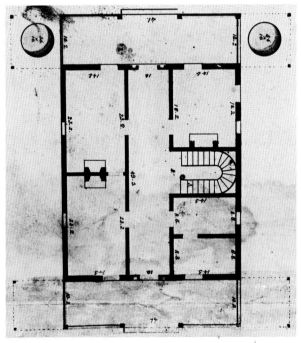

Michael Maher House, Carrollton, 1835–36, drawing by Henry Mollhausen, 1845, an "American" house in the suburbs of New Orleans featuring a front-facing gable roof, center passage, and elliptical fanlights. *New Orleans Notarial Archives*

III. *The Louisiana Plantation House—Two Traditions*

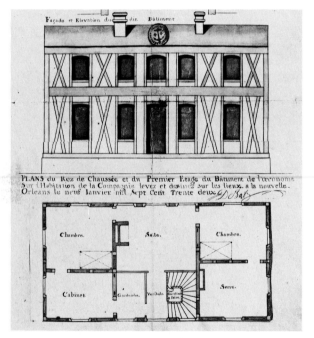

Earliest surviving drawing of a Louisiana plantation house, built outside New Orleans in 1732, designed by Alexandre deBatz without the galleries that later become a characteristic feature of Louisiana plantation houses. *Archives de France*

In the early 1750's, the French-born planter Jean dePradel was supervising construction of a new house at Mon Plaisir, his plantation across the Mississippi from New Orleans.[1] The plan for this building, to be "one hundred sixteen feet in length by forty-eight in width *including the galleries which will surround the house,*" was obtained from the French engineer Alexandre deBatz, whom Pradel later disparaged as being "too much of a drunkard." Pradel's dwelling was a traditional Louisiana plantation house of the late 18th and early 19th centuries, consisting of a single principal story of frame construction, raised on a brick basement, surrounded by wide galleries, and covered with a tall hipped roof. Typically, this house was longer in plan than it was deep, most often consisting of a single file of rooms, to facilitate cross ventilation. Pradel's galleries were twelve feet wide, with 336 feet of "solid balustrade all around" and columns "made according to the orders of architecture and painted like white marble." Pradel exclaimed in a letter to his brothers in France in May, 1751: "What a great convenience these galleries are in this country!"

Pradel's plantation workers manufactured the planks, shingles, and bricks, but the hardware, glass, paints, mirrors, tables, and tapestries came from France. The salon was twenty-four feet wide, twenty-six feet long, and fourteen feet high, with paneled walls, four "large and fine" windows, and two doors, five feet wide, "all well glazed and polished." This salon was furnished with four mirrors hanging over consoles with marble tops and gilded pedestals, another mirror over the chimneypiece, a tapestry, armchairs covered with crimson velvet, and a large sofa with a clock hanging above it. "Although we may be in another world than France," Pradel wrote, "we like our comforts and we give ourselves our conveniences as best we can." The house at Mon Plaisir was engulfed by the Mississippi in the early 19th century, and the surviving wing was destroyed when Confederate powder stored in it blew up in 1861.

Unlike Pradel's comfortable house, the earliest buildings of Louisiana were boxlike structures ill suited to the torrid Southern climate. The earliest known plan of a Louisiana plantation house, built in 1732 for the manager of the Company of the Indies outside New Orleans, conspicuously lacked provision for cross ventilation and those other features that later became so characteristic of houses in the area by the end of the 18th century. It took at least a generation for the Frenchmen who came to Louisiana, like the Englishmen who had come to South Carolina in the late 17th century, to learn how to adapt to the climate. Then, like Pradel's building, houses would be increased in length but not in depth to allow cross ventilation, raised on foundations that elevated them above the marshy soil and frequent floods, and surrounded by galleries that shaded the exterior walls. These galleries also replaced interior hallways, so stairs were often placed on the open galleries and not inside the dwelling. It was not until 1749, fifteen years after its initial construction, that galleries were added to the Company of the Indies manager's house. François Broutin's 1749 drawing for a building for the chief civil officer of the colony featured two-tiered columned galleries across the front and rear elevations. But a scholarly study of Natchitoches, one of the earliest settlements in Louisiana, suggests that there were few, if any, galleries built on houses in that area before 1758.[2]

Historians can trace easily the changes of architectural styles, but it is much harder, often impossible, to detail the evolution of architectural forms. The origins of the gambrel roof or log cabin—or the galleried plantation houses of Louisiana—are so remote and undocumented that they can only be guessed. Scholars have found parallels to the galleried plantation houses of Louisiana in Canada, France, and the West Indies as well as in the Mississippi Valley as far north as Illinois. Though cultural geographers have mapped with precision the areas of Louisiana where French language, law, customs, and architecture have prevailed—the land along the Mississippi, the Red River, and the bayous of the south—it is still unclear whether the galleried plantation houses of Louisiana reflect persistent French influence, brought by early colonists from Canada, France, or the West Indies, or represent a shared attempt by colonists in many places to protect the walls and windows of their buildings from sun and rain. The idea of galleries may have been brought to Louisiana, not direct from France or Canada, but by way of the West Indies, when trade with the Caribbean islands increased in the third quarter of the 18th century.[3]

In any case, records of Louisiana plantation houses with galleries and elongated plans multiply after 1763, when Spain's control of Louisiana began and Caribbean trade increased. In the late 1760's, a raised plantation house with brick basement and galleries was to be built for Claude

Louisiana, showing areas of French culture along the banks of the lower Mississippi, the Red River, and the bayous of the South.

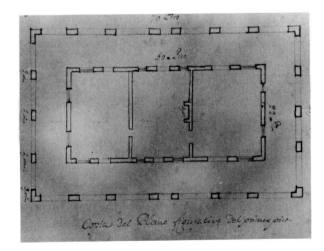

House of Claude Dubreuil, outside New Orleans, c. 1770, the builder's original plan. *Rosamonde E. and Emile Kuntz Collection, Manuscripts Department, Tulane University Library, Gift of Felix H. Kuntz*

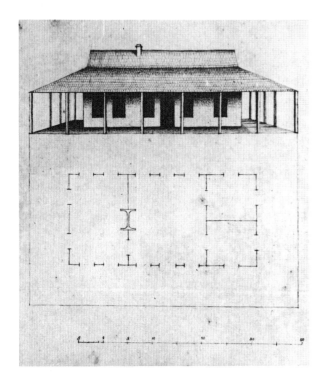

Spanish Commandant's House, Baton Rouge, 1788. *Historic New Orleans Collection*

Pierre deMarigny House, New Orleans vicinity, late 18th century, detail on a map of New Orleans by Vinache. *Historic New Orleans Collection*

Dubreuil outside New Orleans. The house was to be fifty feet long and twenty-two feet deep, surrounded by a gallery ten feet wide raised on masonry piers. The interior was divided into three rooms by two walls, which were built of timber filled with brick. Another house with an elongated plan and surrounding galleries was built in 1788 for the commandant of the Spanish garrison at Baton Rouge. In the late 18th century a large plantation house with a gallery was built downriver from New Orleans for the sugar planter Pierre deMarigny. The house was used as a residence for the last French administrator of Louisiana, Pierre deLaussat. It was from the gallery of this house that the artist John Boqueta deWoiseri painted his famous view of New Orleans, illustrating many houses with galleries. An early sketch of the Marigny house, made before its demolition about 1806, carefully records the robust urn-shaped colonettes and delicate scroll brackets of the gallery.

Not surprisingly, considering the prosperity that came to Louisiana at the end of the 18th century, the oldest surviving houses date from the Spanish, not the French, period. The house at Destrehan plantation, on the east bank of the Mississippi in St. Charles Parish above New Orleans, was built in 1787–90 for Robert deLogny by a free black carpenter named Charles. The building contract describes "a house of sixty feet in length, by thirty-five in width . . . raised ten feet on brick piers with a surrounding gallery of twelve feet in width." Destrehan was enlarged for the first time about 1820 when wings were added for Jean d'Estrehan, deLogny's son-in-law, and again remodeled about 1840 when the original colonettes on the gallery were enclosed within Tuscan columns. However, the original plan and fenestration were retained, as well as the wildly sloping roof. Also in St. Charles Parish is another house of the same general form: Ormond, built in the 1790's with wings added about twenty years later.

Although family tradition relates that Parlange, near New Roads, Pointe Coupee Parish, was built in the mid-18th century for Vincent deTernant, details of the interior and window transoms suggest a construction date of 1795–1810. Except for the front stairs, which were added in the mid-19th century, Parlange represents the perfect idealization of the traditional Louisiana plantation house. Homeplace, built for Pierre Gaillard about 1801, stands on the west bank of the Mississippi near the village of Hahnville, St. Charles Parish. About 1900 two rear chimneys and an original stair under the front gallery were removed. The present stair descending from the front gallery is modern, but an original stair under the rear gallery remains in place. Elmwood, which once stood on the east bank of the river in Jefferson Parish, was probably built for Norbert For-

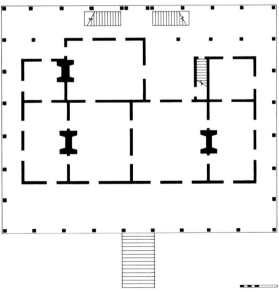

Parlange, New Roads, c. 1795–1810.

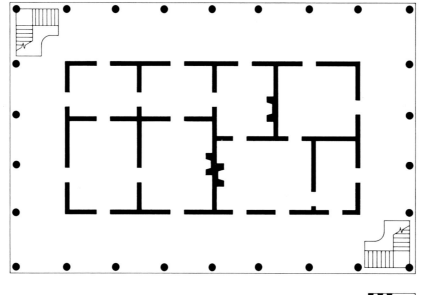

Homeplace, Pierre Gaillard House, Hahnville, c. 1801.

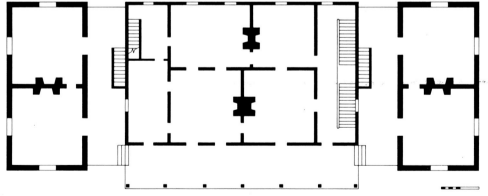

Ormonde, St. Charles Parish, c. 1795, wings added c. 1815. *Louisiana State Museum*

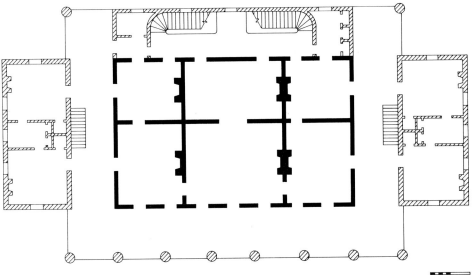

Destrehan, Robert deLogny House, St. Charles Parish, 1787–90, wings added
c. 1820, Tuscan columns added c. 1840.

tier soon after he inherited the land upon his mother's death in 1804. Elmwood burned in 1940.[4] Another large, galleried plantation house belonged to Pierre de la Ronde in St. Bernard Parish below New Orleans. Built about 1805, de la Ronde's house was seventy-five feet long and forty-two feet deep, plus galleries. De la Ronde's house burned in the 1880's.[5]

In 1803, a French settler named Charles Robin recorded his impressions of a tour along the Mississippi outside New Orleans: "As one leaves the city, it is rare to find panes in the windows even a few miles away. Often the hinges and even the locks are of wood, and the houses may not have a single nail in them." Robin found many *cabanes*, huts of the same type built by colonists a century earlier, with walls of traditional *bousillage* construction: "Cypress posts about three inches square and about ten to fourteen feet long are driven into the ground a depth of about two feet, to form the shape of the house. The roof truss and joists are pegged to these posts and hold the house together. The vertical posts are slatted and the chinks filled with earth mixed with Spanish moss. . . . The roofs of the houses are covered with bark, with planks or with shingles. . . . The doors are . . . made entirely without iron, not even a nail. Bolts, locks, even the keys, are made out of wood. The chimney . . . is made of four posts tilted inward toward each other, with slats nailed across the posts, the whole covered with a wide coat of mud." Robin observed that larger houses had elongated plans, galleries, and *bousillage* construction: "Some of the houses are of brick with columns, but the usual construction is of timber with the interstices filled with earth, the whole plastered over with lime. These houses have ordinarily only two or three large rooms, but the heat of the climate makes galleries around the houses a necessity."[6]

James Cathcart, an Irish-born sailor sent to survey timber for naval construction, described similar traditional buildings at St. Martinsville in 1819: "Some few houses are in part built of brick, but mostly of Mud. . . . The houses which are built of mud, is mix'd with moss, with which every tree is nearly cover'd up. It is put up by hand, without the use of the trowel, on shelves place[d] from one frame to the other, and becomes very hard & strong, when thoroughly dry, some plaster over, some white wash only, & the poorer class leave them in their original state, owing to the scarcity of lime, their only resource being to bring clam shells from the Lakes, or Oister [sic] shells from the Sea shore to make it of. Their doors & joiners work are done in the crudest manner, & few houses of the last description have any glass in the windows."[7]

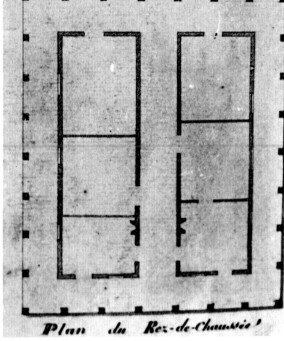

Madame Laurence Bertrand House, Clouet Street, New Orleans, c. 1836. *New Orleans Notarial Archives*

Country builders also continued to erect traditional cottages with raised basements and galleries. In 1803, when Pierre deLaussat, the last French colonial official, reached Natchitoches, where the French had established a fort on the Red River about 1714, he was told by the planter Emmanuel Prud'homme that the settlers of the area "mixed very little and are French in heart and blood." The house at Oakland plantation, three miles southeast of the village of Natchez, Louisiana, was built in 1818–21 for Jean Pierre Prud'homme, whose grandfather Jean had come from France in the early 18th century. A similar house, elevated on a brick basement with galleries and hipped roof, is Oaklawn, built for Narcisse Prud'homme in 1830–35. Dormers in the roof were removed in 1952. A few miles to the south, the house at Melrose plantation was built in 1833 for Louis Metoyer, grandson of a French soldier and a freed slave. Hexagonal wings were added about 1907–11. Melrose is owned by the Association of Natchitoches Women and is open to the public.

Closer to cosmopolitan New Orleans, where "American" newcomers from the East were bringing the tastes of New York and New England, the traditional Louisiana plantation house was adapted to the Federal style. Madame Laurence Bertrand's house, built on Clouet Street in the outskirts of New Orleans about 1836, had three features missing from earlier traditional houses of this type: a plan that was now deeper than wide, a long central hall with interior staircase, and a wide fanlight entrance.[8] Sarpy, built on the east bank of the Mississippi in St. Charles Parish near present-day Norco about 1830, also featured a delicate fanlight and rigid symmetry. Both of these examples have been demolished.

In the late 1820's, Southern builders began to experiment with monumental porticoes and colonnades. The Pentagon Barracks at Baton Rouge was designed by James Gadsden, an army engineer who later earned fame as negotiator of the Gadsden Purchase from Mexico. Built in 1819–24, four barracks and a warehouse were arranged to form a pentagonal enclosure within a star-shaped fortification. Galleries with monumental Tuscan columns shaded walls overlooking the pentagonal lawn. Similar columns and galleries were added to the outer walls in 1834. The wings of Centenary College at Jackson, with two-story Tuscan columns, were designed by Richard Delafield, an army engineer from New York City, and built in 1832–33. Another army engineer, Frederick Wilkinson from Poughkeepsie, New York, designed the New Orleans Barracks in 1833. Built in 1834–35, the Barracks also featured galleries with monumental Tuscan columns.[9] The East Feliciana Courthouse at Clinton, designed by J. L. Savage and built by Lafayette Sanders in 1839–40, is surrounded by a peripteral colonnade.[10] Perhaps these builders were inspired by the

Sarpy, Norco vicinity, c. 1830. *Historic New Orleans Collection*

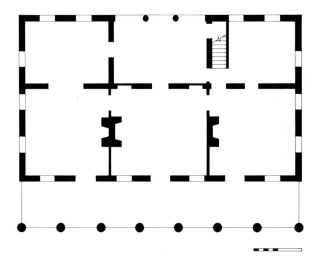

Shadows-on-the-Teche, David Weeks House, East Main Street, New Iberia, 1831–34.

monumentality of the Greek Revival, which had already begun to spread to the Deep South from Philadelphia and New York.

The Shadows-on-the-Teche, on East Main Street in New Iberia, was built in 1831–34 for the sugar planter David Weeks, son of an English-born father who had come to West Florida as a refugee after the American Revolution. Probably because of Weeks's non-French background and cosmopolitan connections, The Shadows—though retaining the traditional arrangement of rooms—featured one of the first monumental domestic porticoes anywhere in Louisiana. In December, 1831, the bricklayer Jeremiah Clark began moulding and burning 256,000 bricks. In 1833 Mary Weeks wrote to her brother Alfred: "My patience is nearly exhausted with waiting so long for a house." In the fall of 1833 and winter of 1834, the carpenter James Bedell was making cellar doors and windows, pediments, sliding doors, a chimneypiece, and thirty-six pairs of sashes and blinds. In the spring of 1834 David Weeks, who had journeyed to Connecticut to improve his failing health, dispatched carpets, furniture, and oil lamps from New Haven. In June, 1834, Mary Weeks wrote her husband: "We have moved into the New House. . . . We are quite snug after great rubbing and cleaning. I never saw a more delightful, airy house, my room particularly. I have all the children in it and open the doors and windows every Night."[11] The Shadows was restored in 1919–22 for Weeks Hall, a descendant of the first owner, who bequeathed it to the National Trust for Historic Preservation. The Shadows is open to the public.

The Shadows may have inspired the design of another house, Chretien Point, near the hamlet of Sunset. Built during the same years and in the same corner of Louisiana, both houses have almost identical plans. Chretien Point, however, has only a simple portico and hipped roof instead of the elegant triglyph-and-metope frieze and gable at The Shadows. In May, 1831, the carpenter Samuel Young and bricklayer Jonathan Harris contracted to complete the new house at Chretien Point for Hypolite Chretien, son of a French-born cotton planter. Three years later, in 1834, Young and Harris built additions to the Academy of the Sacred Heart at nearby Grand Coteau.

Although sophisticated architects from New York began creating buildings in the new Greek taste in New Orleans during the early 1830's, country builders, especially in the areas of early settlement along the rivers and bayous of lower Louisiana, continued to favor Roman architecture. As Benjamin Latrobe observed, old-fashioned builders, trained by apprenticeship, continued to plod along in their old habits. The mansion house at Evergreen plantation, on the west bank of the Mississippi

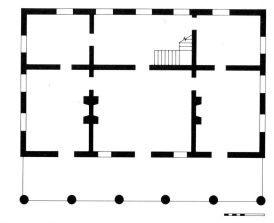

Chretien Point, Hypolite Chretien House, Sunset vicinity, 1831–32.

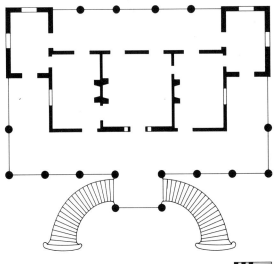

Evergreen, Christophe Haydel House, Vacherie vicinity, c. 1795, portico, columns, and elliptical entrance added in 1832. *Louisiana State Museum*

Oak Alley, Jacques Telesphore Roman House, Vacherie vicinity, 1837–39. *Photograph by Frances Benjamin Johnston, Library of Congress*

six miles downriver from Vacherie in St. John the Baptist Parish, was built for Christophe Haydel in the late 1790's and remodeled for his grandson, Pierre Clidamant Becnel, in 1832. In April, 1832, the builder John Carver agreed to pull down the old roof, raise the second story two feet, and add an octagonal rooftop pavilion with benches and a "Chinese" roof. John Carver also contracted to add a narrow projecting Tuscan portico, an elliptical doorway and sidelights, described in the contract as a "Venetian door," and "two winding stairs gracefully wind[ing] down with the proper slope."[12] The transformed Evergreen is particularly interesting in the overall history of Louisiana architecture, for it was one of the few attempts to reconcile the traditional galleried house with the altogether different concept of a projecting pedimented portico. Evergreen was restored in 1944.

Evergreen has monumental columns arranged with surprising refinement, but Oak Alley has a magnificent colonnade of twenty-eight monumental Tuscan columns that completely surround the building. Oak Alley plantation, located near Vacherie, takes its name from the 800-foot-long avenue of oak trees leading from the river to the mansion, which was built in 1837–39 for Jacques Telesphore Roman by George Swainey. It has been suggested that the design might have been provided by Roman's father-in-law, the French architect Joseph Pilié, but no documentation has been found. The dormer windows were added during a renovation of the house in 1925–26.

About 1840, the owner of Houmas House in Ascension Parish, John Preston Smith, added new front rooms and a monumental Tuscan portico to the front and sides of a house built in the early 19th century. The twenty-four Tuscan columns that surround The Hermitage, outside the village of Darrow, also in Ascension Parish, are believed to have been added about 1840 to a house of 1812–14. Other houses with monumental colonnades were built at Three Oaks plantation in St. Bernard Parish, Seven Oaks plantation in Jefferson Parish, and Uncle Sam plantation in St. James Parish. Uncle Sam commands particular interest, for the great mansion was flanked by other buildings with colonnades. Built in 1843–49 for the French-born sugar planter Samuel Fagot, the buildings at Uncle Sam were demolished in 1940. It is important to remind ourselves that majestic columns do not alone constitute the Greek Revival and, though they may have been inspired by the monumentality of the Greek Revival, the ideal of these builders remained the traditional plantation house with galleries, not the pedimented Greek temple, and the details of these buildings were Roman, not Greek.

The Hermitage, Darrow vicinity, 1812–14, colonnade added c. 1840. *Photograph by Richard Koch, Southeastern Architectural Archive, Tulane University, Bequest of Richard Koch*

Three Oaks, St. Bernard Parish, c. 1840. *Louisiana State Museum*

Seven Oaks, Jefferson Parish, c. 1840. *Louisiana State Museum*

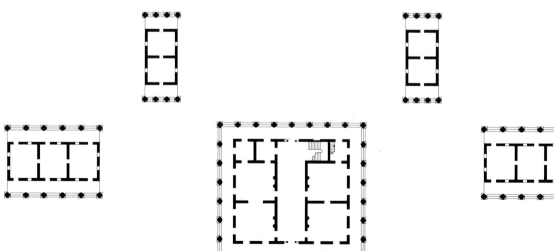

This page and opposite: Uncle Sam, Samuel Fagot House, St. James Parish,
1843–49, with a plan showing arrangement of colonnaded plantation buildings.
Library of Congress

Plate 26 of Minard Lafever's *Beauties of Modern Architecture* (New York, 1835), model for the parlor doorcase at Bocage. *Private Collection*

Two sophisticated mansions built on the east bank of the Mississippi in the early 1840's for members of the Bringier family marked, at last, the adaptation of the traditional Louisiana house to the Greek Revival. Marius Bringier came from Provence to Louisiana by way of the sugar island of Martinique in the late 18th century and established himself as a rich indigo, sugar, and cotton planter. Marius's son-in-law Christophe Colomb lived at Bocage, on the east bank of the Mississippi two miles above Burnside in Ascension Parish. A traditional house with galleries built in the early 19th century, Bocage was substantially rebuilt about 1840, soon after Colomb's marriage to François Bringier, with correct Greek Revival details copied from books. Plate 26 of Minard Lafever's *Beauties of Modern Architecture*, published at New York just five years earlier, was used as the model for the parlor door frames, and Plate 21 was copied for the parlor centerpieces. Much American domestic architecture during the early 19th century was designed with the aid of published illustrations of doors, windows, mantels, or whole houses. Thus, these books were vital to the spread of sophisticated styles from cities to countryside. Significantly, these books were rarely used in Louisiana, outside of New Orleans.

Ashland, near Geismar, on the east bank of the river sixty miles above New Orleans, was built in 1840–41 for Marius Bringier's granddaughter, Nanine, and her husband, Duncan Kenner, soon after their marriage in May, 1839. Kenner, a sugar planter who was the eighth-largest slave-owner in Louisiana, was sent to Europe at the close of the Civil War in a desperate, last-minute effort to barter recognition of Southern independence in return for the abolition of slavery. Ashland is surrounded by twenty-eight monumental pillars, each three feet square. Despite its superficial resemblance to the traditional Louisiana house, Ashland has a wide central hall and the principal living floor on the ground story. The interior of Ashland has been gutted, but still intact are parlor centerpieces copied from Lafever's Plate 21.

In the following decade, Louisiana builders in the areas of early settlement continued to adapt the traditional house to successive tides of fashion. The house at San Francisco plantation, at Reserve in St. John the Baptist Parish, was built for the Louisiana-born sugar planter Edmond Marmillion between 1852, when an earlier house was destroyed by a break in the levee, and 1856, when Marmillion died. Although it has a traditional elongated floor plan without a central hall and with *cabinet* rooms, San Francisco's eclectic and imaginative wooden ornament transform it into a Romantic villa. San Francisco is open to the public. Philip Porcier-Zenon Trudeau House, which formerly stood on the east bank of

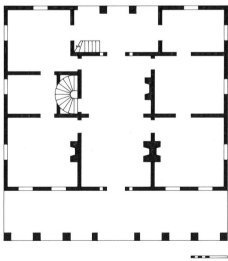

Bocage, Christophe Colomb House, Burnside vicinity, early 19th-century house, remodeled about 1840.

Parlor doorcase, Bocage.

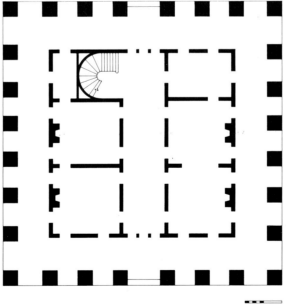

Ashland, Duncan Kenner House, Geismar vicinity, 1840–41. *Louisiana State Museum*

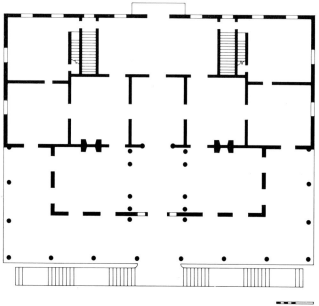

San Francisco, Edmond Marmillion House, Reserve vicinity, c. 1852–56.

Painted folding doors at San Francisco plantation.

Philip Porcier-Zenon Trudeau House, Convent vicinity, c. 1850. *Photograph by Frances Benjamin Johnston, Library of Congress*

the Mississippi outside the village of Convent, was another house with the traditional elevated basement and galleries, the design enriched with sawnwork ornament and octagonal *cabinet* rooms enclosing ends of the galleries. Similarly, the greatest Gothic house of Louisiana, Afton Villa, created in the early 1850's for David Barrow, the wealthiest planter of West Feliciana Parish, is best understood as an attempt to adapt the traditional Louisiana house to the pointed arches and clustered columns of the Gothic style (see pages 163–166).

Meanwhile, a separate architectural tradition, brought by frontiersmen from the upper and coastal South, was evolving in areas of Louisiana beyond the old French and Spanish settlements. Reducing a complex cultural phenomenon to an oversimplification, this was a tradition that came from England by way of the Atlantic seaboard, instead of France by way of the Caribbean. East and West Feliciana, two parishes located on the east side of the Mississippi, were transferred to England by France at the end of the French and Indian War in 1763 and were not incorporated into the Louisiana Territory until 1810. As the province of West Florida, the Felicianas became a refuge for unreconstructed Tories after the Revolution and were settled principally by Virginians and Carolinians. Settlers from the Carolinas and Georgia, with smaller numbers from Tennessee and Kentucky, flooded into the northern parishes of Louisiana in the 1830's, when former Indian lands were at last opened to settlement and the New Jersey-born engineer Henry Shreve began to clear the Red River above Natchitoches for navigation. The hilly landscape and the buildings of the eastern and northern parishes recall the rolling piedmont of North Carolina, South Carolina, and Georgia.

Log houses were known to the French in Canada and therefore were not unknown to the French in Louisiana, who called them *maisons pièce sur pièce*. Their log buildings were, however, more compact and more carefully made than those thrown up hastily by the Scotch-Irish settlers of northern Louisiana, where the largest concentration of surviving log houses can be found.[13] In southern Louisiana, where *bousillage* construction endured, log buildings never became typical, as they did elsewhere along the American frontier.

Frontiersmen in the South were not unskilled, but they were in a hurry. Timber-frame construction used square timbers, fitted together in a complicated pattern with wooden pegs, a painstaking and slow process. Log buildings were made by laying logs—mostly pine and some oak in northern Louisiana—horizontally, fitting them together at the corners with simple notched joints, so that each log was held in place by the weight of the log above it. The log house may have wasted wood, which was plen-

Undocumented 19th-century log house, Keithville vicinity, c. 1840. *Photograph by Goodloe R. Stuck*

tiful in the frontier, but it saved labor, which was scarce. Window openings, if any, were left unglazed and closed only by shutters. Gaps between the logs were covered with horizontal boards nailed to the inner surface of the logs or filled with clay and sticks. In January, 1844, Mary Marshall, a settler who had come from South Carolina to DeSoto Parish, wrote to her father: "We, the children and myself, walked to the bayou and brought home plenty of myrtle and pine to dress the house with. Grandmother remarked that a log house is much more convenient than a plastered one, for you can stick the bushes in the cracks instead of having the trouble of having to put up nails."[14]

Except for the one-room house, the most widespread cabin was made by building two log rooms and connecting them with a wide, open passageway, which served as a sitting and dining room. Frederick Law Olmsted, the veteran Southern traveler and landscape designer from New York, visited such a house in Louisiana in the early 1850's: "The house was a double log cabin, two log erections . . . joined by one long roof, leaving an open space between. . . . Our room was open to the rafters. . . . The wind rushed at us with a fierce swoop."[15] Olmsted described the contents of another nearby log house, which consisted of only one room twenty feet wide and sixteen feet long: a big four-post bed, a camp bed beside it, a table, a dresser filled with crockery, a bureau, two deer-skin chairs, and a Connecticut-made rocking chair.

Despite the moonlight and magnolia mythology that has obscured the plain reality of Southern life, the vast majority of Southern farmers lived in modest comfort but without much display. Even wealthy farmers put their money in land and slaves, not in big houses. The typical farm house of the Old South was a two-story, gable-roofed building with exterior end chimneys, center hall, a shed front porch and shed rooms at the rear. Many early frame houses retained the most distinctive feature of log houses: the wide, open central passage. The undocumented Colvin House, which once stood outside Vienna in Union Parish, was such a house. Surviving houses of this type are numerous in East Feliciana Parish, many of them built by settlers from Georgia and the Carolinas when they arrived in the first decades of the 19th century. The house at Oakland plantation, outside Gurley, was built about 1827 for Thomas Scott, a settler from South Carolina, with renovations about 1840. Its wide central hall, which can be completely opened to the outside by pairs of folding doors at both ends, echoes the open passages of double log cabins from a generation earlier. But chimneypieces carved with delicate sunbursts reflect the Adam-Federal style that was making its way even to the frontier from seaport cities in the East.

Colvin House, undocumented, Vienna vicinity, featured an open center passage.
Photograph by Richard Koch, Southeastern Architectural Archive, Tulane University Library, Bequest of Richard Koch

Palladian houses illustrated in William Halfpenny's *Useful Architecture* (London, 1752) and Robert Morris's *Select Architecture* (London, 1757). *Avery Architecture and Fine Arts Library, Columbia University*

Restored elevation of Thomas Andrews House, Clinton, 1830, by James S. Cripps and Frank Masson.

In the late 18th and early 19th century, English traditions inspired the building of a group of small farm houses in Virginia and North Carolina. Like a Palladian villa, these buildings featured a two-story central block, its gable facing forward to form a templelike pediment, flanked by one-story wings. This idea created grandeur on a small scale and provided cross ventilation and natural light in each of the principal rooms. We can follow the spread of this idea from illustrations in 18th-century English books to builders in Virginia and North Carolina and then to settlers moving toward the Southwest across the Southern piedmont, in South Carolina and Georgia in the 1820's, and in Alabama, Mississippi, and Louisiana in the 1830's. The 1830 house of Thomas Andrews, a settler from South Carolina, at Clinton must have been created by especially skilled artisans, itinerant craftsmen or new settlers from the states along the Atlantic coast. This building, with its distinctive form brought from the upper South down the piedmont over three generations of migration to an area of Louisiana settled principally by Carolinians and Georgians, is a textbook example of how buildings are three-dimensional history books, dramatizing how people carried these architectural traditions with their other baggage across the frontier. Long known as the Chase House, the Thomas Andrews House was demolished in 1960, although some fragments were re-erected on another site.

In 1800, the widow Olivia Barrow and her three surviving children came from Halifax County, North Carolina, by way of Tennessee to West Feliciana Parish. The house at Rosedown plantation outside St. Francisville was built in 1834–35 for a Barrow granddaughter, Martha, and her husband, the Scottish-born cotton planter Daniel Turnbull. Their builder was Wendell Wright, a contractor for the new Woodville-West Feliciana Railroad. Wright agreed to complete "the carpenter and joined work . . . after the most modern stile, the front to be executed with full gretio dorric collums and cornice."[16] In his journal, Daniel Turnbull recorded that work on his house commenced in November, 1834, and was completed in May, 1835. Wings were added in 1844–45. Rosedown's gable roof, low foundation, and two-tiered Doric portico recall houses in the piedmont of North Carolina. Rosedown is open to the public. William Ruffin Barrow, the older brother of Martha Turnbull, ordered construction of an even grander house at nearby Greenwood plantation about 1835. The design of its peripteral Doric colonnade is attributed to James Hammon Coulter, a coffin-maker and carpenter from Delaware. Greenwood burned in 1960 but has been reconstructed on its original site. Coulter is also believed to have built a house at Ellerslie plantation near Tunica in the late 1820's for William Wade, a North Carolina-born judge who married a member of the Barrow family.

Thomas Andrews House, Clinton, 1830. *Photograph by Richard Koch, South-eastern Architectural Archive, Tulane University Library, Bequest of Richard Koch*

Rosedown, Daniel Turnbull House, St. Francisville vicinity, 1834–35.

During the Greek Revival the temple became an idealized and widely admired form in America. Though builders in the areas dominated by French culture continued to build long houses with surrounding galleries, simply substituting monumental Tuscan columns for slender colonettes, builders in the eastern and northern parishes preferred the narrower form of the pedimented temple. After the 1836–37 Union State Bank at Clinton was purchased by Henry Marston, a Boston-born merchant who had come to East Feliciana Parish in 1822, he was delighted to convert the building into his residence, because its templelike design seemed as appropriate for a house as for a bank.[17] Nearby, the David Davis House, long known as the Braeme-Bennett House, was built at 227 South Baton Rouge Street for a physician from Virginia in 1839–42. Davis's builder ran a pediment from the end of the gable and a complete entablature with triglyphs and metopes along the cornice to form a frieze, making this small house into a diminutive Greek temple. Far to the north in Claiborne Parish, farther away from French influence, the undocumented, now-demolished Bonner House, built about 1845, featured a two-story Doric portico flanked by one-story colonnaded wings.

Union State Bank/Henry Marston House, Clinton, 1836–37. *Louisiana State Museum* .

The Pugh family, including the brothers Whitmel, Augustine, and Thomas, moved from Albemarle County, North Carolina, to Bayou Lafourche near Napoleonville about 1820 and, before the Civil War, amassed thirteen plantations employing more than 1,300 slaves. The Pughs were three of the earliest "Americans" in an area of predominantly French settlement and must have surprised the neighborhood when they employed the New York-trained architect Henry Howard to build their plantation houses in the late 1840's. Henry Howard (1818–1884) was born at Cork, Ireland, the son of a local builder from whom he received a knowledge of mechanics and the rudiments of drawing.[18] He sailed to New York at the age of eighteen in 1836 and worked in a picture-frame factory for eight months before joining his brother, a builder named Benjamin who had already come to Louisiana, at New Orleans. Reaching there in late 1837, Henry was employed as a carpenter and stair-builder and as a foreman by Edward W. Sewell, builder of the St. Louis Hotel. Howard also worked for James Dakin and Henry Mollhausen and opened his own office about 1846. Between 1857 and 1860 Howard worked in partnership with Albert Diettel. Diettel (1824–1896) was born in Dresden and worked as a mason and railroad engineer before coming to New Orleans by way of New York in 1849.[19]

About 1846 Howard prepared designs for Thomas Pugh's Madewood plantation near Napoleonville, featuring a two-story Ionic portico flanked by one-story wings with hyphens. About 1849 Howard remodeled the

David Davis House, 227 South Baton Rouge Street, Clinton, 1839–42.

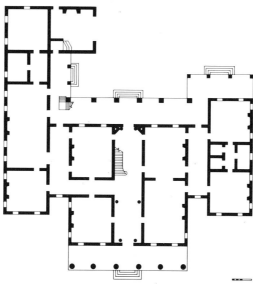

Madewood, Thomas Pugh House, Napoleonville vicinity, c. 1846.

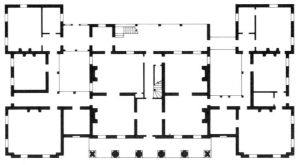

Woodlawn, William Pugh House, as remodeled c. 1849. *Library of Congress*

Insane Asylum, Jackson, 1847–55. *Louisiana State Museum*

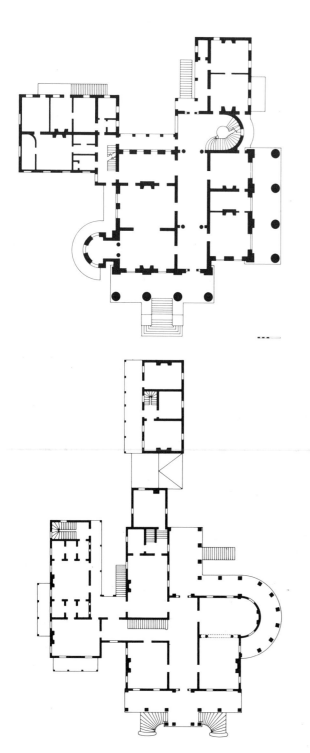

Plans of Belle Grove, top, and Nottoway, bottom, both by Henry Howard for neighbors at White Castle, Louisiana, in the 1850's.

house at nearby Woodlawn plantation, home of Thomas Pugh's nephew William, adding a two-story Ionic portico and masonry wings to the older frame structure. The house at Woodlawn was demolished in 1946. The Ionic order was a special favorite of Howard, for he also employed it at the Jefferson Parish Courthouse, 719 South Carrollton Avenue in New Orleans, in 1854–55, the St. Martin Parish Courthouse at St. Martinville in 1854–59, and the central building of the Insane Asylum at Jackson. Begun in 1847, the commanding center building of the Insane Asylum—with the only three-story pedimented portico in Louisiana—was designed by Henry Howard, with wings by Charles Gibbons, and completed in 1855.

Between 1852 and 1855 Howard was occupied with the design and construction of the mansion at Belle Grove, near White Castle, for the sugar planter John Andrews. With an assymetrical plan and lavish materials and ornament in a style we might call Romantic Classicism, the house at Belle Grove, long a ruin, burned in 1952.

Howard and his partner Albert Diettel also designed a plantation villa for Andrews's neighbor, the Virginia-born sugar planter John Hampden Randolph.[20] Even after the Civil War, Randolph retained seven thousand acres of land on four plantations in Louisiana. In June, 1857, Howard and Diettel agreed to complete the drawings and specifications for Randolph's house at Nottoway, to hire the workmen and superintend construction. Principal craftsmen included the Irish-born carpenter Timothy Joyce, painters New York-born Henry Sequin and Eugene Carraine, plasterer William J. Supple, and glazier Henry Pamart. In August, 1859, Howard wrote to the vexed Randolph: "I regret to learn . . . of the great trouble you have had with Mr. Joyce. I . . . would suggest the propriety (for your own benefit) to allow him to finish his contract with you. At this season of the year it is almost impossible to employ good Carpenters. . . . I intend to write to Joyce and give him a severe blowing up. You do not deserve any trouble from his hands."[21] Luxurious details of the house include a gas works, ten pin alley, and two large water tanks under the roof. Nottoway is open to the public.

Belle Grove, John Andrews House, White Castle vicinity, 1852–55. *Photograph by Frances Benjamin Johnston, Library of Congress*

Belle Grove, interior view. *Photograph by Richard Koch, Southeastern Architectural Archive, Tulane University Library, Bequest of Richard Koch*

Nottoway, John Hampden Randolph House, White Castle vicinity, 1857–59.

IV. *The Greek Revival*
James Gallier & James Dakin

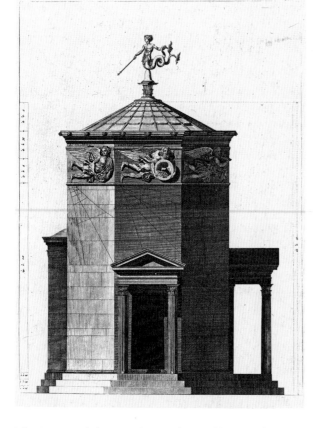

The Tower of the Winds at Athens, illustrated in the first volume of *Antiquities of Athens* (London, 1762) by James Stuart and Nicholas Revett. *New York Public Library*

The Mississippi and its tributaries carried the products of about 25,000 miles of navigable waterways to the lap of New Orleans. The port's waterfront was lined with ships, two and three deep, the tops of their masts seen as a forest over the levee. On the levee itself there were stacks of cotton bales and a lively parade of swaggering boatmen, half-naked Indians, and manacled slaves. By 1840 the population, which had been 49,000 in 1830, doubled once again to 102,000. New Orleans, the third-largest city in the nation and second only to New York in importance as a port, had now supplanted the great 18th-century city of Charleston, South Carolina, as the metropolis of the South.

The advent of the Greek Revival to Louisiana coincided with the flood of new talent coming to New Orleans. Despite its association with the young nation's democratic ideals and with the great white columns of the Old South, the Greek Revival was neither particularly American nor particularly Southern. The road from Athens to New Orleans traveled by way of Paris, London, Philadelphia, and New York. An English publication, James Stuart and Nicholas Revett's *Antiquities of Athens,* the first three volumes of which appeared between 1762 and 1794, illustrated the ancient monuments that became icons of 19th-century Greek architecture. The English-born architect Benjamin Latrobe, who called himself "a bigoted Greek," designed the first Greek portico in the Old Southwest on an octagonal brick engine house for the New Orleans waterworks in 1810. The Greek Revival first came to Philadelphia in the late 1790's. William Strickland, the architect from Philadelphia who designed the United States Mint at New Orleans in 1835, once wrote: "The student of architecture need go no further than *The Antiquities of Athens* as a basis for design." James Dakin, an architect from New York who worked in Louisiana for eighteen years, designed a fire station in New Orleans in 1841 with a fantastic cupola modeled on two of the ancient buildings featured in Stuart and Revett's *Antiquities,* the 4th-century Choragic

James Dakin's June, 1841, design for the Louisiana Hose Company, New Orleans, featured a fantastic cupola modeled on the Tower of the Winds and the Choragic Monument of Lysicrates. *New Orleans Public Library*

Methodist Church, 619 Carondelet Street, New Orleans, featured a tall cupola also modeled on the Choragic Monument of Lysicrates. *Louisiana State Museum*

Monument of Lysicrates and the 1st-century Tower of the Winds. Dakin may have been the designer of the 1851–52 Methodist Church at 619 Carondelet Street, with its tall cupola also modeled on the Choragic Monument of Lysicrates.

Among the many newcomers who came to New Orleans during this period of spectacular growth were architects and builders from the North—and from New York City in particular.[1] In 1819, Benjamin Latrobe's complaints about impractical Yankee designs in New Orleans were cut short by "an American bricklayer" who told Latrobe that he had "all New York in my favor."[2] In 1833 the Massachusetts-born missionary Timothy Flint noted that, among the Americans in New Orleans, the New Yorkers seemed to be the greatest in number. Of 2,301 architects, builders, contractors, carpenters, and joiners living in New Orleans in 1850, only 23 percent were born in Louisiana and 7 percent came from other Southern states, while 25 percent were born in Europe, 24 percent in Britain and Ireland, and 11 percent came from the Mid-Atlantic states, 5 percent from New England, and 3 percent from the Midwest.

The full flowering of the Greek Revival came to Louisiana in the 1830's, introduced to New Orleans by architects and builders from New York City. Except for Benjamin Latrobe's Doric portico on the 1811 waterworks engine house, and also the Doric arcade on Jean Baptiste Thierry House designed by Latrobe's son Henry in 1814, the first use of the Greek orders was the New Orleans Canal and Banking Company on Magazine Street, built in 1831 by John Reynolds of Philadelphia and James Zacharie from Maryland to the design of Richard Delafield from New York.[3] Delafield (1798–1873) was the son of an English-born merchant whose family intermarried with the powerful and aristocratic Livingstons and became one of Wall Street's richest bankers. Richard graduated from West Point in 1818 and was then ordered to Louisiana to build fortifications at Fort Jackson on the Plaquemine Bend of the Mississippi near New Orleans, where he worked between 1824 and 1832. It is easy to imagine how Delafield, talented son of a famous banker who was enjoying the society of New Orleans, would have been asked to design the Bank. Delafield also devised a canal, financed by the bank, between the Mississippi and Lake Ponchartrain. The granite-sheathed Bank was distinguished by an elegant one-story Doric portico and flamboyant consolelike gables flanking the attic story. In 1843–45, the Canal Bank was enlarged by James Dakin, who retained Delafield's original Greek portico. The Canal Bank, 301 Magazine Street, was recently renovated. During the Civil War, Delafield commanded the engineering office of the United States Army in Washington.

The Choragic Monument of Lysicrates, also known in the 18th century as Demosthenes Lanthorn, illustrated in Stuart and Revett's *Antiquities of Athens* (London, 1762). *New York Public Library*

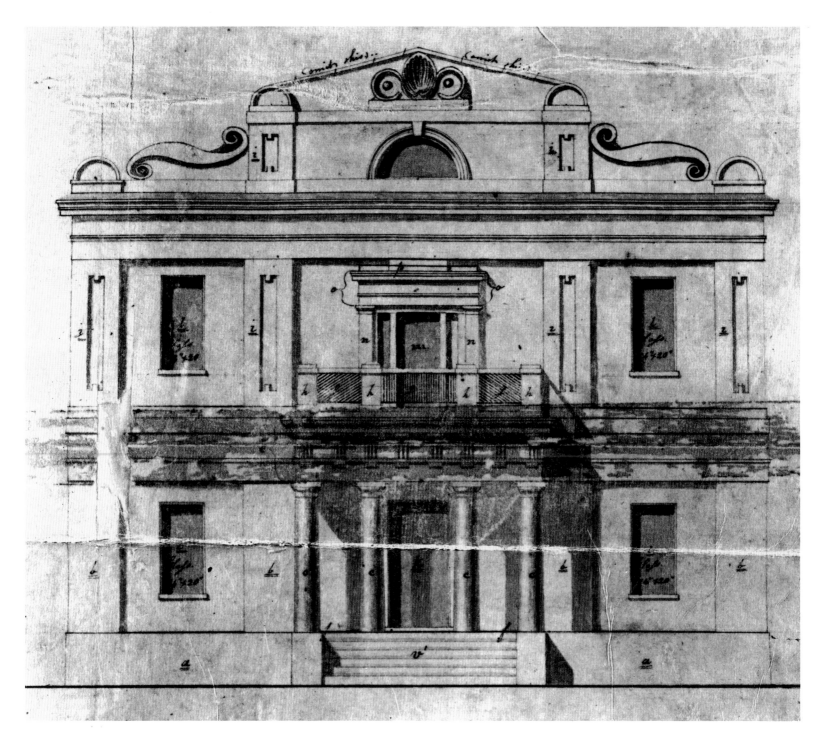

Canal and Banking Company, New Orleans, design by Richard Delafield, 1830.
New Orleans Notarial Archives

Another architectural talent from New York City who brought the Greek Revival to New Orleans was the Scottish-born George Clarkson. Clarkson (1809–1835) came to New Orleans about 1832, at the age of twenty-three, to help build row houses designed by the New York architects Ithiel Town and Alexander Jackson Davis and their new partner James Dakin for the New Orleans Building Company, which had been chartered in 1828 to erect houses and offices in the American district. Clarkson produced a few houses and two important public buildings before an early, violent death. The Commercial Bank, with a monumental Ionic portico, was built on Magazine Street in 1832–33 by Daniel H. Twogood. The First Presbyterian Church on Lafayette Square, with a recessed Doric portico, was built in 1834–35. The minister, Joel Parker, was born in Vermont, educated in New York City, and traveled to New England to raise money for the Church's construction. The Commercial Bank has been demolished, the Presbyterian Church burned in 1854. In July, 1835, at the start of a most promising career, Clarkson was stabbed to death during a street brawl by another architect who came to New Orleans from New York in the early 1830's, Alexander T. Wood.

In 1835 the United States Congress authorized construction of three branch mints at Charlotte, North Carolina, Dahlonega, Georgia, and New Orleans.[4] The mints at Charlotte and New Orleans were designed by William Strickland (1788–1854), one of the most successful first-generation professional architects in America. Born in New Jersey, Strickland had been introduced to Benjamin Latrobe by his father, a country carpenter working on Latrobe's 1798 Bank of Pennsylvania, the first example of Greek architecture in the young nation. Strickland studied with Latrobe for three years. In 1819 the authorities in Washington accepted Strickland's design for a new Custom House at New Orleans; it is believed that his drawings were the ones used for the Custom House completed in 1820. The New Orleans Mint, built in 1835–38 on Esplanade Avenue, has an E-shaped plan with a projecting central portico and wings terminating in pediments. Like the United States Naval Asylum at Philadelphia, 1826–33, and the United States Mint at Philadelphia, 1839–43, both designed by Strickland, the Mint at New Orleans features a broad Ionic portico flanked by long wings.[5] The builders were the brickmason John Mitchell and carpenter Benjamin F. Fox. Strickland moved to Nashville, Tennessee, in 1845 to supervise construction of his Tennessee State Capitol. There he died nine years later. The architects James Gallier, Jr., and James Dakin were later hired at different times to strengthen the Mint by adding brick arches and iron rods. The Mint served its original purpose until 1910 and was restored by the State of Louisiana in the late 1970's.

Commercial Bank, Magazine Street, New Orleans, 1832–33. *Historic New Orleans Collection*

First Presbyterian Church, Lafayette Square, New Orleans, 1834–35. *Louisiana Collection, Tulane University Library*

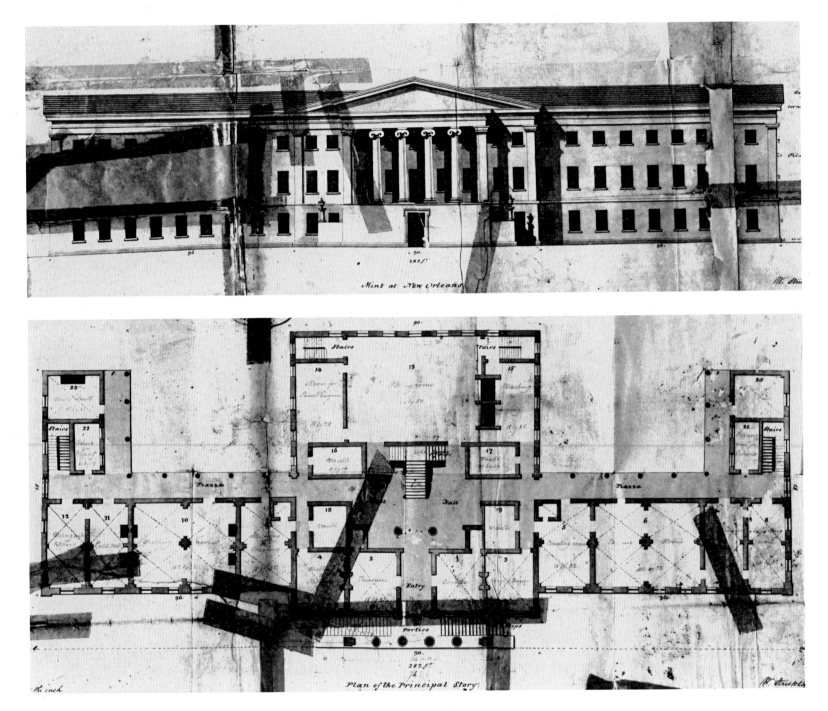

United States Mint, New Orleans, design by William Strickland, 1835. *New Orleans Notarial Archives*

United States Mint, Esplanade Avenue, New Orleans, 1835–38, a 19th-century
photograph. *Louisiana State Museum*

In the mid-1830's, three gifted young architects who had worked in New York City—James Gallier, James Dakin, and his brother Charles Dakin—decided to seek professional opportunities in burgeoning New Orleans. James Gallier, born in Ireland in 1798, the son of a builder, studied architectural drawing in Dublin and, while working with his father, "filled up every spare hour I could get at copying the orders of architecture."[6] In 1822, at the age of twenty-four, Gallier moved to London with his brother John, who later followed him to America. In London Gallier worked at odd jobs in the building trades for four years, until he was employed by William Wilkins, the veteran architect and author of *Antiquities of Magna Graecia*, an 1807 folio that surveyed Greek sites at Aegesta, Selinus, Paestum, Sicily, Syracuse, and Agrigentum. An early drawing has survived for houses that Gallier designed in London about 1830 for a Mr. Robson in Park Street. In 1832 Gallier sailed to New York where he worked first as a draftsman for James Dakin and later became a partner of the New Jersey-born architect Minard Lafever. He provided drawings of a Greek villa for the frontispiece of Lafever's *Modern Builder's Guide*, published at New York in 1833. In the same year Gallier, always the doughty Irishman, presented in Brooklyn a series of public lectures on architecture. Two of the seven lectures were devoted to Greek architecture.

James Dakin (1806–1852) and his brother Charles Dakin (1811–1839) were born in Dutchess County, New York, and both worked for the famous New York Greek Revival architects Ithiel Town and Alexander Jackson Davis. James Dakin, trained by his guardian, a country carpenter named Herman Stoddard, was a gifted artist who was later praised by Gallier as "a young man of genius."[7] James Dakin provided drawings for ten plates in Minard Lafever's *Modern Builder's Guide*. In 1830 James Dakin became a partner of Town and Davis. As early as 1832 Town, Davis, and Dakin were providing designs for houses that were to be built in New Orleans.

Meanwhile, as he later recounted in his spirited memoirs, Gallier had heard that New Orleans offered great opportunities for young architects "if I could only bear the climate."[8] Also realizing the demand for new buildings in New Orleans, James Dakin may have persuaded his enterprising friend Gallier and his younger and less-talented brother Charles to go there as his agents to work as architects and builders. In October, 1834, Gallier and Charles Dakin sailed to New Orleans. After several weeks of delay at Mobile, Alabama, where they waited out one of Louisiana's recurrent yellow fever epidemics, they set up an office on Canal Street in New Orleans and "hung its walls with plans and drawings."[9]

Design of commercial building for William Mortimer, New Orleans, by Alexander Jackson Davis, c. 1831. Davis's diaries mention that he designed other buildings in New Orleans, including a store for William Montgomery in August, 1830, another store for Anthony Rarch in June, 1832, and a hotel in March, 1835. *Metropolitan Museum of Art*

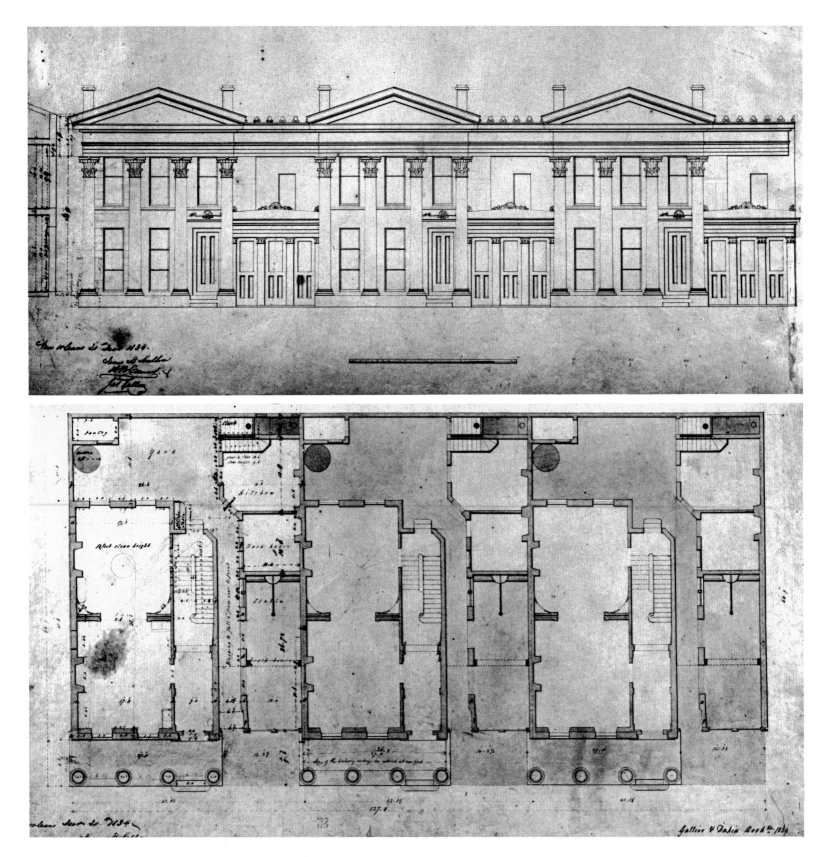

The Three Sisters, a row of three houses on North Rampart Street, New Orleans,
drawing by James Gallier, Sr., December, 1834. *Labrot Collection, Southeastern
Architectural Archive, Tulane University Library, Gift of Sylvester Labrot*

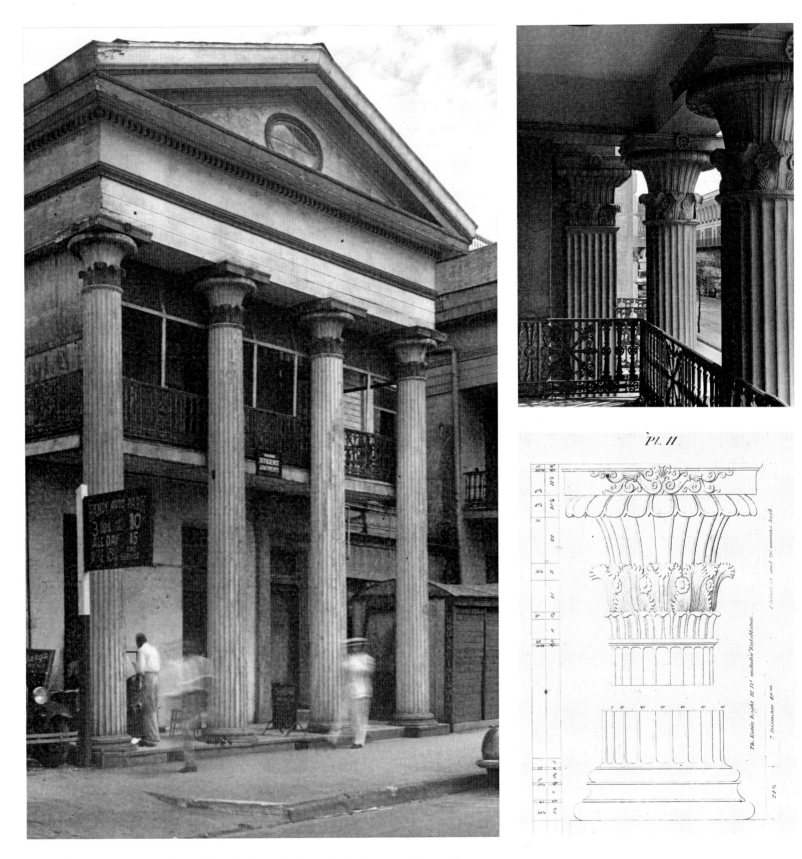

The Three Sisters, portico and capitals, with the model, Plate 11 of Minard Lafever's *Beauties of Modern Architecture* (New York, 1835). *Portico photograph by Richard Koch, Southeastern Architectural Archive, Tulane University Library, Bequest of Richard Koch; photograph of capitals by Richard Koch, Gallier House, Tulane University; Lafever plate from private collection.*

Study by James Dakin for a large public building with an Ionic portico, c. 1835.
There is also a sectional view of the interior of Christ Church in the New Orleans
Public Library drawn by James Gallier, Sr. *New Orleans Public Library*

Gallier and Charles Dakin, introduced to the sympathetic Northern-born leaders of the city's American district, many of them clany Irishmen, found a rich and eager clientele.

Soon after their arrival, in December, 1834, Gallier and Charles Dakin produced drawings for a row of three houses on North Rampart Street. This ingenious design featured three monumental porticoes linked by recessed hyphens, and so the houses were soon dubbed The Three Sisters. The design was further distinguished by Tower-of-the-Winds capitals, a detail probably provided by Gallier or James Dakin, both of whom had worked for Minard Lafever and may have drawn the Tower-of-the-Winds capital for Plate 11 of Lafever's *Beauties of Modern Architecture*. A note on one of the drawings for The Three Sisters indicates that the balcony railings were ordered from New York. The last surviving house in the row was demolished about 1950.

In the spring of 1835, Gallier and Charles Dakin designed the Arcade Baths on Camp Street for the Irish-born theatrical impresario and entrepreneur James Caldwell. This long, narrow building, adjacent to two theaters owned by Caldwell, contained a coffee house and twenty-four public baths on the first story, a ballroom and billiard room on the second story, and forty-two lodging rooms for gentlemen on the third and fourth stories.[10] The original design featured an opulent Corinthian portico bearing a sculptural sea goddess astride a giant fish, but during construction the portico was replaced with simple pilasters. The Arcade Baths opened in October, 1836, and burned in 1842.

When the octagonal brick church designed by Henry Latrobe in 1816 began to collapse in the summer of 1835, the vestrymen of Christ Church employed Gallier and Charles Dakin to produce plans for a new building at the corner of Canal and Bourbon streets. Their design for a dignified Ionic temple was approved in July, the walls were raised to the roof by December, and the Church was completed in the summer of 1837 by Daniel H. Twogood, builder of the row of houses on Julia Street designed in 1832 by James Dakin.[11] One parishioner, Joseph Lovell, complained that Christ Church looked more like a bank than a church. The design recalls undated studies made by James Dakin in New York before coming to New Orleans. The second Christ Church became a synagogue in the late 1840's and was demolished in 1857.

By March, 1835, Gallier and Charles Dakin—with the probable assistance of James Dakin in New York—produced designs for a Merchants Exchange to be built on Royal Street in 1835–36. The builder was again Daniel H. Twogood. The austere granite façade was enlivened by windows set between giant pilasters so they appeared visually as a single

Christ Church, Canal Street, New Orleans, 1835–37, detail from a lithograph by Jules Lion, 1840. *Louisiana State Museum*

Merchants Exchange, Royal Street, New Orleans, 1835–36, illustrated in a city directory of the period. *Louisiana Collection, Tulane University Library*

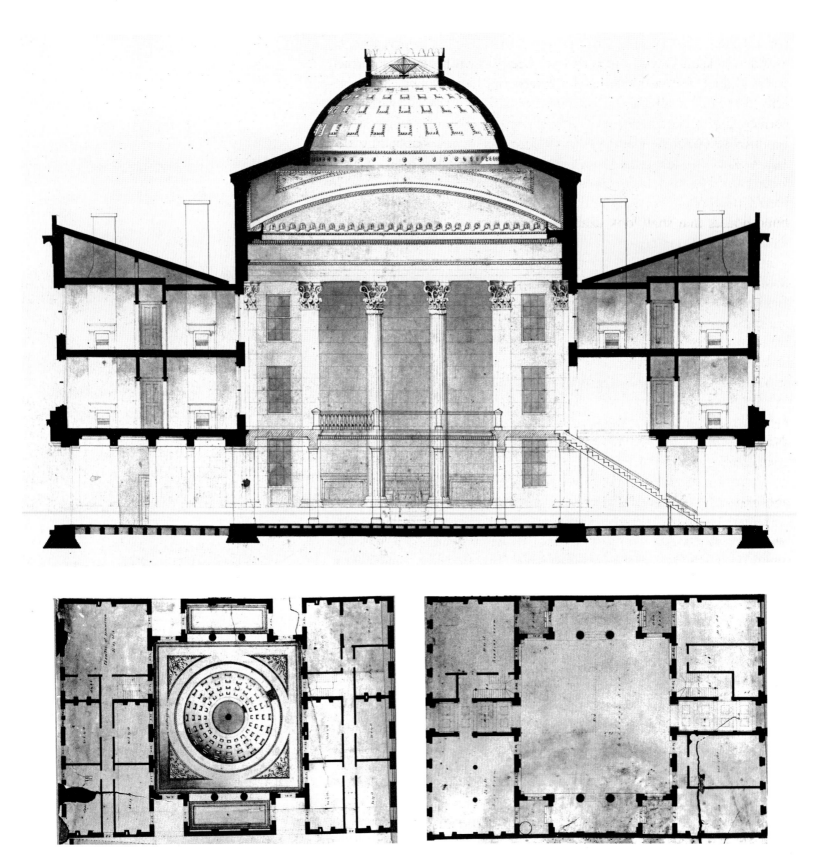

Merchants Exchange, sectional view and plans of first and second stories, by James Dakin, c. 1835. *Sectional view from Historic New Orleans Collection, plans from New Orleans Public Library*

vertical shaft. They were called "Davisean" windows by their creator, Alexander Jackson Davis, and may have been drawn by Davis's partner, James Dakin. The visitor entered a three-story-high trading room, lavishly decorated with Corinthian pilasters and columns, an anthemion cornice, and a flattened dome with a skylight. Though unsigned, the beautiful sectional view of the Exchange interior was probably drawn by James Dakin. A less-gifted rival builder may have had Dakin in mind when he condemned Yankee architects as "picture-makers" who come to New Orleans and "get a high price for their drawings and large wages to build houses that shall look exactly like the picture."[12] The Merchants Exchange burned in 1960.

In April, 1835, the commissioners of the new St. Charles Hotel announced that they had in hand "the drawings and specifications of Messrs. Gallier and Dakin."[13] The architects appear to have been guided by the illustrations in W. H. Eliot's *Description of the Tremont House,* published in 1830, for the 1828–29 Tremont House in Boston and the 1835 St. Charles Hotel in New Orleans share several features.[14] Both were designed to accommodate eccentric trapezoidal sites and employed bays at the ends of each building to disguise awkward corner angles. Also common to each building were interior courtyards, stairs ascending to rotundas, and dining rooms in rear wings. Though Gallier claimed that the St. Charles was principally his own design, James Dakin probably provided its most prominent feature—the magnificent dome that rose 185 feet above the city. In May, 1835, the commissioners advertised for a foreman and hired Michael Collins, an Irishman who later became Gallier's partner in the building business.[15] Most of the carpentry and iron was prepared in the North, and granite was shipped from the quarries at Quincy, Massachusetts.[16] Guests at the Hotel began registering in February, 1837, though the St. Charles was not entirely open until May, 1838.

The St. Charles was as opulent as its promoters promised, at the time of its completion the largest and grandest hotel in the nation.[17] The building was 235 feet long and 203 feet deep. The visitor ascended granite steps, beneath a four-story-high Corinthian portico, to a recessed terrace, up twelve more marble steps into a grand salon in the center of the building. He could detour down to the ground story, where there was an octagonal barroom, seventy feet wide, and fourteen public bathing rooms with hot and cold water, shops, and a wine cellar. The principal story contained a dining room for gentlemen, 129 feet long, with two ranges of Corinthian columns, a ladies parlor, and a second dining room, fifty-two feet long, and kitchens. The visitor could follow a spiral stair up to a circular room under the dome, which was surrounded by an eleven-foot-

St. Charles Hotel, New Orleans, 1835–38, lithograph by Thayer and Company, Boston, 1845. *Louisiana State Museum*

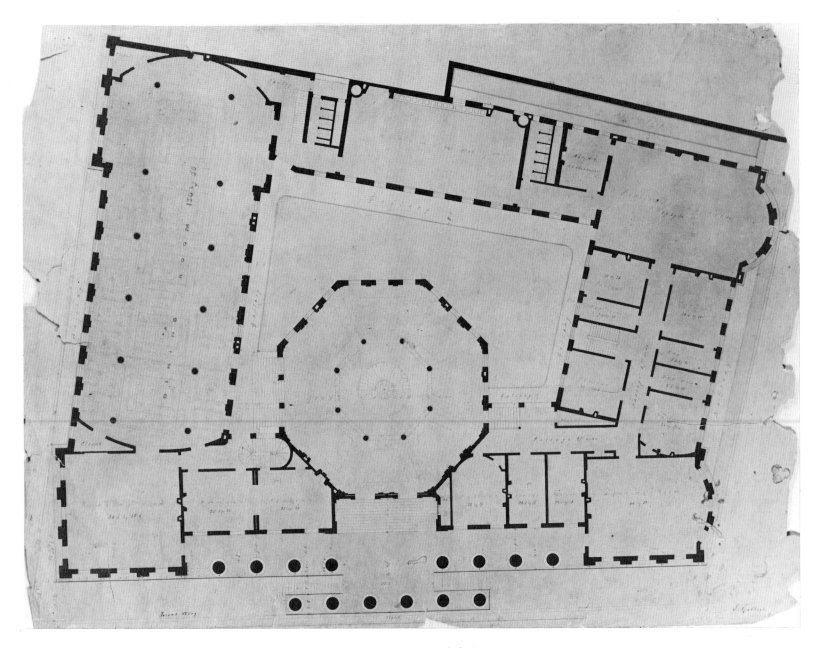

Plan of principal story of St. Charles Hotel, signed by James Gallier, Sr., c. 1835.
There is a similar plan at Southeastern Architectural Archive, Tulane University
Library. *Historic New Orleans Collection*

St. Charles Hotel, St. Charles Street, New Orleans, 1835–38, a unique view of the
hotel with its dome before the building burned in 1851, a daguerreotype by
Thomas Easterly. *Missouri Historical Society, which expressly retains all copyright
to this image*

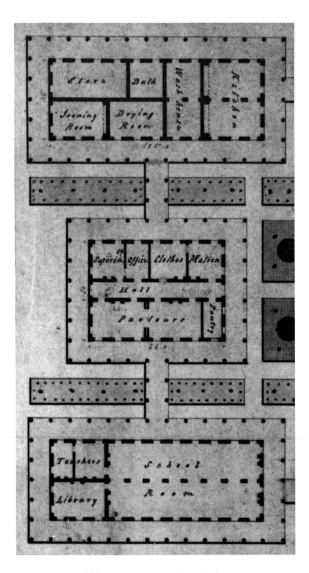

Plan of the Orphan Boys Asylum, New Orleans, by James Gallier, Sr., c. 1839. *Labrot Collection, Southeastern Architectural Archive, Tulane University Library, Gift of Sylvester Labrot*

wide gallery from which he could enjoy panoramic views of the city. There were four stories with 350 bedrooms.

In January, 1851, the St. Charles Hotel burned. "The flames rushed up the lofty dome and the light airy cupola. The upper passages filled with dense, stifling smoke. The flames burst forth from the roof and came out the upper windows . . . whilst the vast interior seemed one raging, blazing furnace. . . . The great dome began to totter. . . . For a moment there was a pause . . . the next instance, cupola and dome fell in, disappearing in a great cloud of smoke and fire!"[18] The directors conferred with James Gallier, Jr., and the Irish-born carpenter Samuel Stewart. They also conferred with Isaiah Rogers, the foremost hotel designer of the era, who came to New Orleans from Cincinnati to prepare estimates for rebuilding in early March, 1851. The building committee finally decided to follow the suggestions of builder George Purves, who proposed using the old foundations and salvaging as much material as possible.[19]

Purves (died 1883) was born in Scotland and came to New Orleans by way of New York in 1847. He designed the Odd Fellows Hall on Lafayette Square in 1849–50, a massive three-story building with Corinthian pilasters and a dome, and the Gothic-style Trinity Church on Jackson Avenue in 1852–53. (The present entrance and tower of Trinity were added in 1873.)[20] Purves was the builder of the Presbyterian Church on Lafayette Square in 1855–56, designed by Henry Howard; the medical school on Tulane Avenue, designed by Howard and Albert Diettel, in 1857; and the F. H. Givens House, St. Charles Avenue, in 1859.[21] In the late 1850's Purves owned a factory that produced doors, sashes, and blinds. The new St. Charles Hotel was completed in 1853, but without the original building's most prominent feature, the magnificent dome.[22] The second St. Charles Hotel burned in 1894.

James Gallier began an independent career as an architect and builder in November, 1835, when James Dakin came to New Orleans and formed a new partnership with Charles Dakin. Four days after James Dakin's arrival, Gallier and Michael Collins, who had been foreman of construction at the St. Charles Hotel, agreed to build a house for William Nott. Gallier's design featured an entrance with an "entablature and square antae . . . in white American marble" and parlors embellished with "two Grecian Ionic fluted columns with carved caps and turned bases . . . of the example from the Ionic temple of the Erectheum at Athens."[23] (An unsigned drawing attributed to James Dakin illustrates similar Ionic columns in a parlor.) In January, 1836, Gallier agreed to build four houses on St. Charles Street for Samuel Moore; in July, he began stores and dwellings on Canal Street for Antoine Jonau.[24] During 1837–38 Gallier

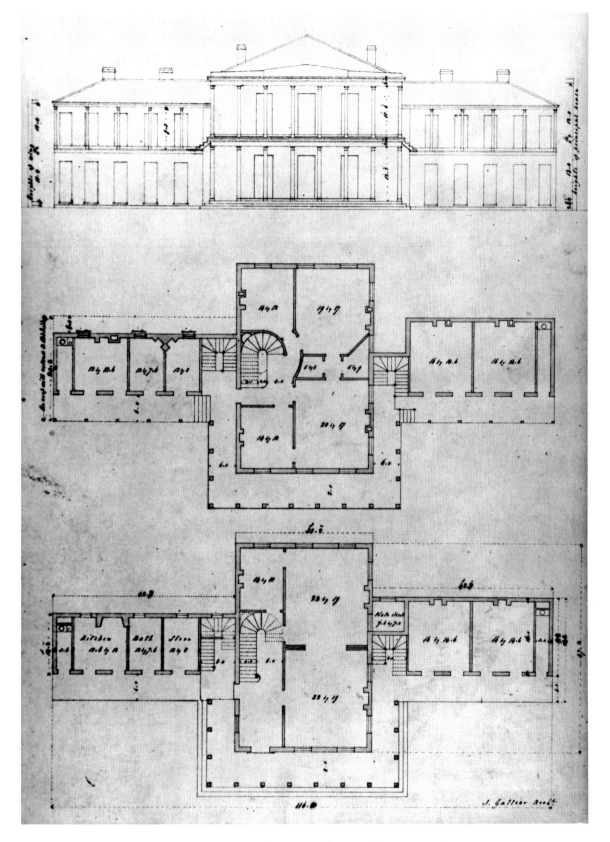

Unidentified villa, drawing by James Gallier, Sr. *Labrot Collection, Southeastern Architectural Archive, Tulane University Library, Gift of Sylvester Labrot*

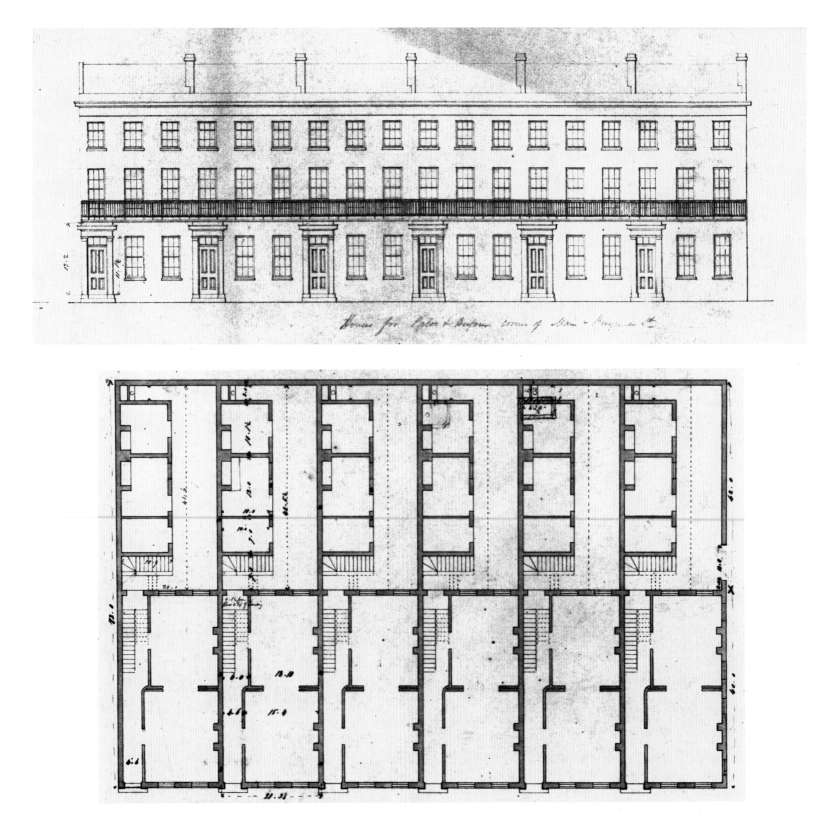

Houses for Hypolite Paloc and Charles Dufour, Burgundy Street, New Orleans,
elevation and plan by James Gallier, Sr., June, 1838. *Labrot Collection, Southeastern Architectural Archive, Tulane University Library, Gift of Sylvester Labrot*

was supervising construction of the City Bank on Camp Street.[25] Designed by W. L. Atkinson in 1836, the City Bank was completed in March, 1838. In May, Gallier designed and agreed to build four houses on Tchoupitoulas Street for Charles Diamont.[26] In June, Gallier completed drawings for a block of six houses on Burgundy Street for Hypolite Paloc and Charles Dufour.[27] The Gallier-Collins partnership ended in 1838.

In 1839 Gallier completed construction of St. Patrick's Church, begun by the Dakin brothers in 1838 (see pages 143–147). About 1839 he submitted designs for an Orphan Boys Asylum. No elevation has been located, but Gallier's grandiose plan, showing three colonnaded buildings, recalls Girard College at Philadelphia, designed by Thomas U. Walter six years earlier. In April, 1840, Gallier designed and agreed to build two stores on Chartres Street for John Hagan, an Irishman who was president of the St. Charles Hotel. In 1841 Gallier worked on drawings for an unidentified house at the corner of St. Charles and Poydras streets. As early as 1841, Gallier began designing an imposing mansion at 824 Canal Street for the prosperous physician William Newton Mercer from Maryland. After returning from Havana in 1842, where he spent several months designing a hotel that was never built, Gallier produced a detailed estimate for Dr. Mercer in April, 1844, and the building contract was signed at the end of May.[28] Since 1883 the Mercer House has been used as a gentlemen's club.

In 1836 the government of New Orleans, long fractured by antagonism between the proud French and the pushy Americans, was formally divided into separate municipalities. A design by the Dakin brothers was selected for a City Hall for the Second Municipality, the American quarter, but construction was delayed by the Panic of 1837. Eight years later, in 1844, the authorities discarded the Dakin design and approved a new one provided by James Gallier. Robert Seaton, a builder from New Jersey who had worked for Town and Davis in New York in 1839–40, began construction in 1846 but quit the work. Gallier himself completed the City Hall in 1851. Granite came from B. F. Dudley of Milton, Massachusetts, and from Wright, Barker and Company of nearby Quincy.[29] The white marble for the portico, surmounted by statues of Justice, Commerce, and Liberty, came from quarries in New York State.[30]

In 1845 Gallier designed a Commercial Exchange on St. Charles Street for sugar brokers, merchants, and sea captains, a three-story stuccoed building with a two-story recessed granite portico of superimposed orders.[31] "It consisted," Gallier wrote, "of one large room on the lower storey, intended for the Exchange; another large and lofty room on the second storey intended for lectures and public exhibitions, and two stories

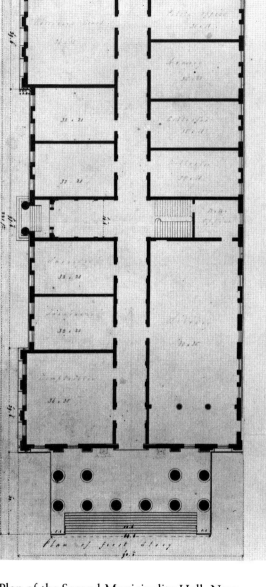

Plan of the Second Municipality Hall, New Orleans, by James Gallier, Sr., 1844. *Labrot Collection, Southeastern Architectural Archive, Tulane University Library, Gift of Sylvester Labrot*

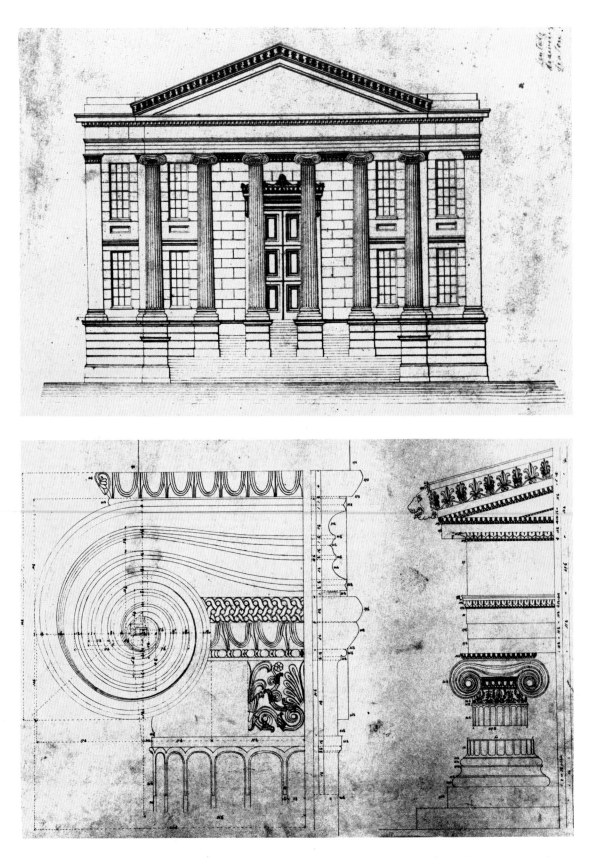

Elevation of Second Municipality Hall and studies of Ionic capitals and entablature by James Gallier, Sr., c. 1844. *Labrot Collection, Southeastern Architectural Archive, Tulane University Library, Gift of Sylvester Labrot*

Second Municipality Hall, St. Charles Street, New Orleans, 1844, a late-19th-century photograph. *Louisiana State Museum*

of rooms on each side for offices."[32] Visitors passed through a narrow vestibule into an exchange room, seventy feet wide, one hundred feet long, and twenty-seven feet high. Gallier acted as builder as well as designer of his Commercial Exchange, which was adapted for use as a Masonic Hall in 1853 and demolished in 1891.

In 1845 Gallier designed a house for the attorney Lucius C. Duncan. In 1846 he revised Thomas K. Wharton's design for a new sanctuary for Christ Church and also undertook its construction (see pages 149–151). In 1847 Gallier built three houses for the cooper James Dick on Dauphine Street, and in 1849 devised alterations to John Hagan's house on Canal Street. He also provided drawings for the Sailors Home, chartered in 1849, a boxy, four-story building that was to be built at the corner of New Levee and Suzette streets. The wings were built in the early 1850's, but the main block was not completed until 1857 by Thomas K. Wharton.

In March, 1849, Gallier sketched preliminary ideas for two row houses for Micaela de Pontalba, the talented, wealthy, and demanding wife of a sugar planter.[33] Madame Pontalba decided to turn the project over to the architect Henry Howard and later to a builder named Samuel Stewart, a forty-eight-year-old Irish-born carpenter. Built by Stewart in 1850–51, using drawings by Howard that were inspired by Gallier's earlier proposals, the Pontalba Buildings are two block-long structures facing opposite sides of the *place d'armes*. Each building is three stories high and comprises sixteen dwelling houses. The façades are enlivened by cast-iron galleries, overlooking the square, and by slightly projecting pedimented pavilions at the center and ends. More interesting is the plan, which perpetuates the traditional "French" idea of open passageways—sometimes a walk, sometimes a carriageway, sometimes a stair—leading to a rear galleried courtyard.

Gallier had been suffering with failing eyesight. In the late 1840's he visited New York and England in an unsuccessful effort to restore his vision. In 1850 Gallier turned over his office to his son, James, Jr. (see pages 169–176). The senior Gallier published a spirited autobiography at Paris in 1864 and died in a steamship wreck in 1866 on a return voyage from Europe.

James Gallier's independent career had begun thirty-one years earlier, in November, 1835, when James Dakin came to join his brother Charles in the booming architecture business in New Orleans. In December, 1835, James and Charles Dakin formed a new partnership, with James, the older and more-talented brother, managing an office at the new Merchants Exchange in New Orleans and Charles representing the brothers in Mobile, where he had already established a reputation among the

Commercial Exchange, St. Charles Street, New Orleans, 1845. *Louisiana State Museum*

Hotel designed by James Dakin and Charles Dakin, to be built facing Lafayette
Square, New Orleans, c. 1835. *New Orleans Public Library*

Union Terrace, Canal Street, New Orleans, 1836–37, an elevation by George T. Dunbar, 1843, and a 19th-century photograph. *Drawing from New Orleans Notarial Archives, photograph from Louisiana State Museum*

Yankee merchants of that Alabama port. The earliest signed drawing by the new Dakin and Dakin partnership is a proposal for a hotel that was to have been built on Lafayette Square in New Orleans about 1835. This design was based on studies that James Dakin had made in 1832 for a hotel in New York. The hotels in New York and New Orleans were never built, but the same general idea of a grandiose structure with a recessed portico, "Davisean" windows, and a dome was developed by the Dakins for the Government Street Hotel that was built in Mobile in 1836–39. Another early project never executed was the plan for a new state capitol, which James Dakin delivered to the legislature in January, 1836. The collection of Dakin drawings at the New Orleans Public Library includes several for a large unidentified building with legislative halls.

In 1836 James Dakin designed Union Terrace, a block of four houses to be built on Canal Street, opposite the old state house, for the insurance company president Richard O. Pritchard, Seamen Field, head of the Merchants Exchange Company, planter Michel Bringier, and merchant William A. Gasquet. Like Town and Davis's LaGrange Terrace in New York, 1832–34, which Dakin may have helped design, Union Terrace in New Orleans, 1836–37, featured a two-story colonnade mounted on the ground story, which serves as a podium. Unlike the conventional squarish block of houses produced by James Gallier for Messrs. Paloc and Dufour in 1838, Dakin's palacelike building had a central semicircular portico flanked by projecting end pavilions. The last house in Union Terrace, having been converted into a theater, was demolished in 1906. Dakin and Dakin also produced another building, the Verandah Hotel, for Richard O. Pritchard in 1836. Completed in 1839, the Hotel featured innovative cast-iron verandahs along the two street façades and a vast dining hall ornamented with "three beautiful elliptic domes."[34] The Verandah Hotel burned in 1855.

In late 1836 James Dakin designed the First Methodist Church, built at the corner of Poydras and Carondelet streets in 1836–37. Like George Clarkson's Presbyterian Church of 1834–35, this was a conventional church of the period in the Greek taste with a recessed Doric portico flanked by pilasters. But James Dakin surmounted the Methodist Church with a daringly incongruous Egyptian steeple. The steeple's cavetto cornice represented in stucco the tops of bushy plants that spilled over the tops of ancient mud walls. The architrave was embellished with ancient religious symbols of the sun disk, cobra, and falcon wings, representing the creation and preservation of life. The columns suggested the stalks of giant lotus plants and the foliage of papyrus plants along the banks of the Nile. The First Methodist Church burned in 1851.

DESIGN FOR DOORS· BETWEEN PARLORS·

Design for Greek interior attributed to James Dakin, c. 1835. *Labrot Collection, Southeastern Architectural Archive, Tulane University Library, Gift of Sylvester Labrot*

In January, 1837, James Dakin proposed an immense public market, with a two-story Corinthian colonnade, fifty-five feet wide and five blocks long, which would have occupied the center of Canal Street. This was the first of several designs for mammoth civic buildings that were never realized because of the Panic of 1837, a national economic collapse caused by speculation, depressed farm markets, and banking uncertainties. A second frustrated venture was the Second Municipality Hall, designed in the winter of 1837 by James Dakin and his new associate, Charles Lagarenne Bell, a draftsman from New York City who had worked for Minard Lafever and provided a design published in Lafever's *Beauties of Modern Architecture*. The design was approved by the city council in March, a building contract was signed in June, and an 1838 city directory described the Hall with confidence: "It will be of the Corinthian order, and the material of white marble. It is to have an 80 foot front, by 170 feet in depth, and will contain all the public offices of the Second Municipality, together with the Commercial Library and two spacious Armories for volunteer companies. The roof is to be surmounted by an elegant Cupola of circular form 150 feet in height." [35] Construction was delayed after the Panic, the Dakin contract was abandoned in 1841, and the authorities finally adopted a different design by James Gallier, Sr., in 1844.

In June, 1837, Dakin, Bell, and Dakin submitted a design for the proposed Marine Hospital for two or three hundred patients that was to be built by the national government at McDonoughville, on the west bank of the Mississippi River across from New Orleans. This design presented a two-story brick building with a raised basement, a U-shaped plan partially enclosed with a screen of monumental Ionic columns, and a slender cupola. Several other designs were submitted, among them one by Antonio Mondelli and his partner John Reynolds. These proposals were rejected in favor of drawings by Robert Mills, the South Carolina-born architect who had recently been appointed Federal Architect by President Andrew Jackson (see pages 143–149).

James Dakin's disappointments continued in the wake of the Panic of 1837. In February, 1839, he proposed designs for a State Library, a chaste Doric structure with a two-story portico flanked by one-story wings. The Library was not built, but Dakin developed the same general idea for a Medical College that was built on the same site four years later. In 1840 Dakin, who had submitted plans for a new Capitol to the legislature in January, 1836, prepared a second design for a building to replace the old Charity Hospital on Canal Street, which had been converted into a state house in 1835. This grandiose plan, with two sprawling buildings and six porticoes, was completely impossible for the straitened finances of the state government.

Dr. Stone's Hospital, Canal Street, New Orleans, 1837–38. *Louisiana State Museum*

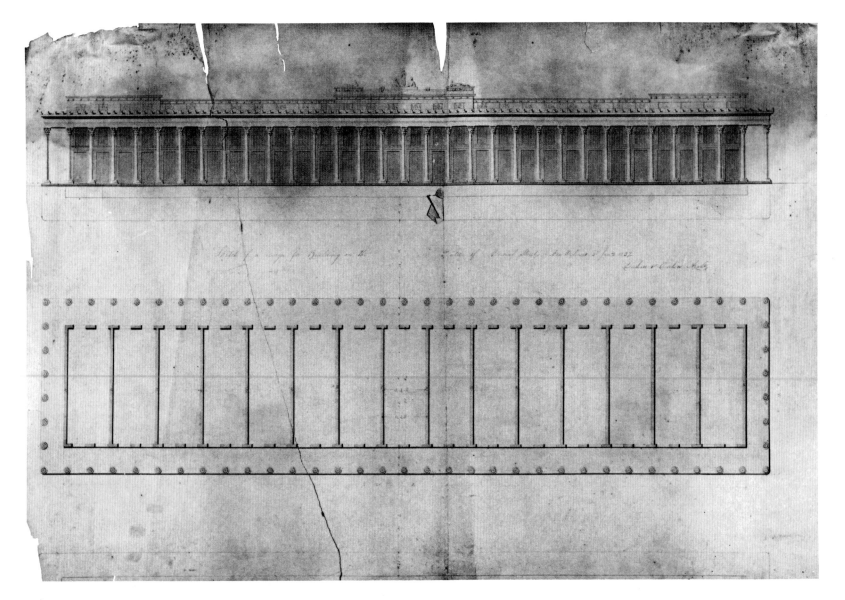

Design for a Public Market, New Orleans, by James Dakin, 1837. *New Orleans Public Library*

Design for Second Municipality Hall, New Orleans, by James Dakin, Charles Bell, and Charles Dakin, 1837. *New Orleans Public Library*

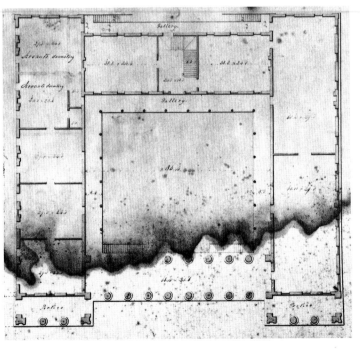

Design for Marine Hospital, New Orleans vicinity, by Dakin, Bell, and Dakin,
May, 1837. *New Orleans Public Library*

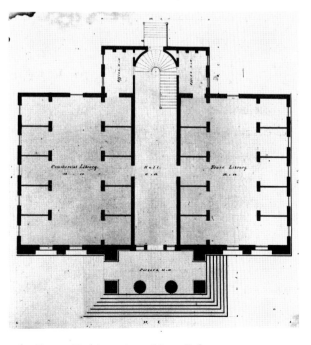

Design for a State Library, New Orleans, by James Dakin, 1839. *New Orleans Public Library*

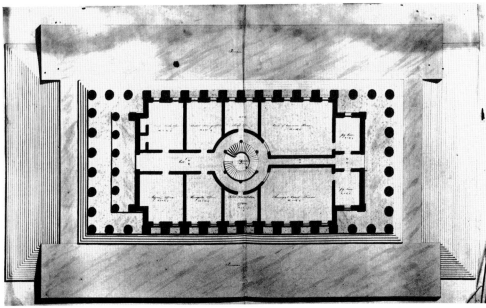

Study for an unidentified public building by James Dakin. *New Orleans Public Library*

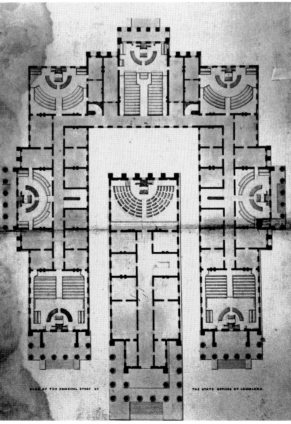

Design for a State Capitol, New Orleans, by James Dakin, 1840. *New Orleans Public Library*

VIEW OF THE STATE ARMORY.

N.O. 1839.

Design for the State Armory by James Dakin, 1839. *New Orleans Public Library*

Far more modest were James Dakin's executed projects of the late 1830's. In 1837 or early 1838 he designed a hospital for Dr. Warren Stone, a Vermont-born surgeon who came to New Orleans in late 1832 and would pioneer the use of ether as an anesthetic in 1847. Built at the corner of Canal and Claiborne streets, then a suburban location, Dr. Stone's Infirmary was one of the architect's least imaginative designs, a boxy, three-story brick building with a massive Doric portico. The Infirmary was demolished in 1883. Between July and October, 1839, the state government erected an Armory on St. Peter Street "to hold 20 pieces of artillery and 10,000 stands of arms." Dakin's austere yet commanding building featured giant pillars, wrought-iron latticework, and "Davisean" windows. Another small but exquisite structure was built on Carondelet Street in 1841 for the Louisiana Hose Company, a volunteer fire brigade. Dakin's witty and cultivated design for the Hose Company tower was adapted from two of the most famous ancient buildings in Athens, the Tower of the Winds and the Choragic Monument of Lysicrates. The Louisiana Hose Company was destroyed in the 1890's.

The building business was so slack in New Orleans that Charles Bell, who had become James Dakin's associate in early 1837, left Louisiana in 1838. His subsequent career is unknown. In 1839 Charles Dakin died, leaving his brother on his own. That summer James was discharged by St. Patrick's Church, for whom he had designed and was building a church (see pages 143–145), embroiling him in a protracted lawsuit. In 1841, suffering from financial reverses in the wake of the Panic of 1837, Dakin declared himself bankrupt. For several months in 1842 he was engaged in designing a hotel in Memphis, Tennessee. In November, 1842, Dakin announced his return to New Orleans and the resumption of his career: "I have again commenced the practice of my profession and will gratefully serve my friends and the public. . . . Every gentleman will find it much to his interest to have plans and specifications of the intended buildings made by a disinterested person before any attempt is made to procure proposals for the execution of the works; because, when the contractors or builders are required, as they very often are, to estimate and make their calculations from verbal explanations and rude sketches, many difficulties and misunderstandings arise. . . . A few dollars paid in the commencement to some architect, who understands his business, will save hundreds in the end."[36]

In March, 1843, the state legislature provided land behind the state house in New Orleans for a new Medical College of Louisiana. Dakin proposed a two-story block with a Corinthian portico flanked by one-story wings. Completed in November, 1843, this building was later

State Armory, St. Peter Street, New Orleans, 1839–40. *Library of Congress*

Study for the University of Louisiana by James Dakin, c. 1847.
New Orleans Public Library

incorporated into a larger building for the University of Louisiana. In December, Dakin undertook the rebuilding of the Canal and Banking Company on Magazine Street. Dakin's design retained the two Doric columns and the entablature of the original portico from Richard Delafield's 1831 building.

The year 1844 was especially busy for Dakin, who was occupied with buildings for Benedict Baggett on Julia Street, for the New Orleans Gas Light and Banking Company on Camp Street, for Andre Millaerts on Jackson Street, for Henry Buckner on Gravier Street, for Eleanor McNeil on Magazine Street, for Lumsden Kendall and Company on St. John Street, for Ann Matthews on Tremé Street, and for the City Bank on Tchoupitoulas Street. In 1845 Dakin undertook buildings for Henry Buckner on St. Charles Street, for Hamilton Wright on St. Charles Street, for Holmes and Mills on St. Charles Street, for Robert Heath on St. Charles Street, and for Rowland Redman on Tchoupitoulas Street.

For several months in 1846, James Dakin was busy organizing and leading a regiment of volunteers to fight in the Mexican War. Upon his return in the spring of 1847, he submitted plans for a new university in New Orleans. The four-year-old Medical College hall would become the left wing of a large E-shaped group of three templelike buildings. The central structure, containing lecture halls, dissecting rooms, a museum, library, and offices, was completed in 1848, and the right wing was completed in 1855. These buildings were demolished in 1898.

In 1845, Congress appropriated $500 for the design of a new United States Custom House to be built at New Orleans.[37] Designs were submitted by at least seven architects, including one from J. N. B. dePouilly, two from James Gallier, and three from James Dakin. Gallier was never paid for his drawings, which were finally returned, soiled and torn. When Dakin saw them at the office of the Collector of Customs, he was not inclined to approve the work of a competitor who had replaced him on two buildings, the Second Municipality Hall and St. Patrick's Church: "I was astonished at the bad taste and worse arrangements of Mr. Gallier's Plan . . . giving no chance for light or air. I consider the whole of them, a lot of rubbish, to speak plain."[38] Dakin also inspected a design that had been submitted by Alexander Thompson Wood (1804–1854), a builder who had come from New York City in the early 1830's to build houses for the Architects Company of New Orleans and then been imprisoned for six years in the state penitentiary after killing his former associate, George Clarkson.[39] Dakin found similar fault with Wood's design for the Custom House: "Mr. Wood's design was a most foolish thing. . . . The entire area of the square was covered, having no means of ventilation or

University of Louisiana, New Orleans, a 19th-century photograph. *Louisiana State Museum*

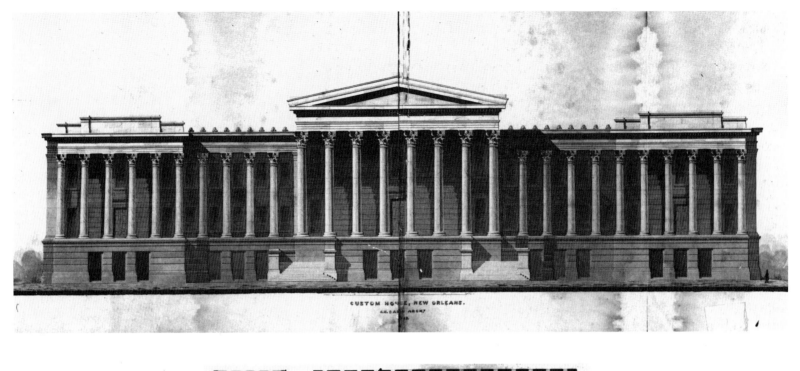

CUSTOM HOUSE, NEW ORLEANS.

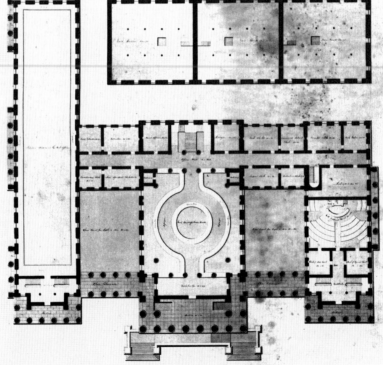

Second design for the United States Custom House, New Orleans, by James Dakin,
June, 1847. *New Orleans Public Library*

air for the interior except by means of a skylight over the General Business Room, which was in the centre of this dense mass of building. His plan would have made a tolerable Mausoleum or Tomb for an Egyptian king!"[40]

Dakin's first proposal, submitted in January, 1846, was a surprising Gothic design (see pages 153–155). He must have been given little encouragement, for in June, 1847, Dakin prepared a second proposal, a grandiose but conventional Greek Revival structure intended to please the expectations of self-important politicians and civil servants. Cleverly exploiting the irregular shape of the site on which the Custom House was to be built, Dakin proposed facing his building toward the river instead of toward Canal Street, with a fountain and garden in a projecting corner of the property. An immense Corinthian colonnade brought unity to a complex design that included four separate buildings for the customs, post office, the Federal courts, and a warehouse for goods in transit. In August, 1847, Dakin made a hasty trip to Washington and New York, where he conferred with Federal officials and drafted a third design, a "perfectly plain" structure intended to satisfy the Treasury Department's request for a large but austere Custom House. Like the chicken and the egg, it is unclear whether the similarities so evident between the Dakin and Wood designs were the result of Wood copying Dakin or Dakin copying Wood—or both copying James Gallier.

Construction of the Custom House at New Orleans began in 1848, with Alexander T. Wood acting as supervising architect of his design. Wood was removed in May, 1850, and James Dakin supervised construction during the summer. When he failed to persuade the authorities to revise Wood's plan by relocating the Business Room on Canal Street—leaving an open court in the center of the building—and by employing structural cast iron in place of masonry arches, Dakin resigned in 1851.

In 1851 and 1852, construction was supervised by Lewis Ethan Reynolds (born c. 1816), a carpenter from Norwich, New York, who had come to New Orleans by way of New York City, Philadelphia, Baltimore, St. Louis, and Washington. In 1843 he opened "a Drawing School . . . drawing of the Orders, Ground Plans, Elevations and Perspective. . . . He has no hesitation in saying that he can teach any carpenter, who is a workman, to do the most complex stairs in two weeks."[41] In 1847 Reynolds was making "Designs and Specifications for Buildings and supervising the erection of the same." In 1849 Reynolds's *Treatise on Handrailing* was published at New Orleans, one of the very few architecture books ever issued in the South. In 1852 and 1853 the supervising architect of the Custom House was English-born Thomas Kelah Wharton.

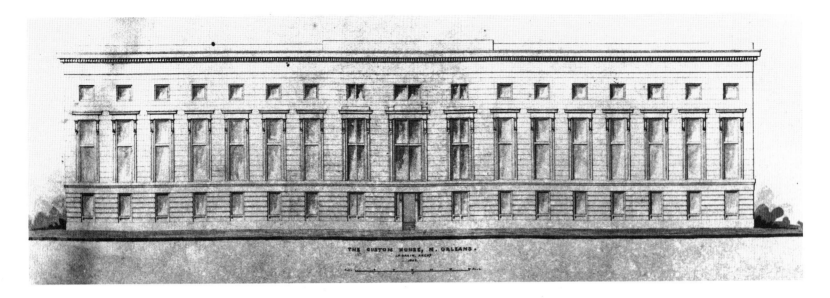

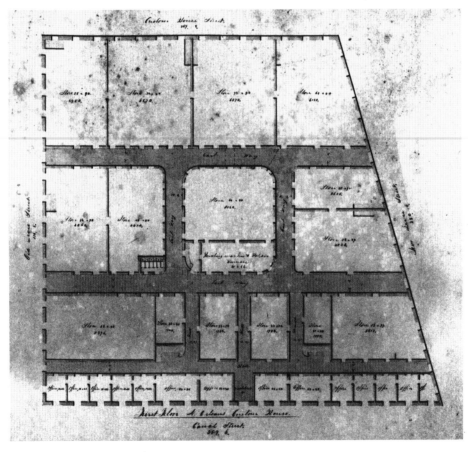

Third design for the United States Custom House, New Orleans, by James Dakin,
August, 1847. *New Orleans Public Library*

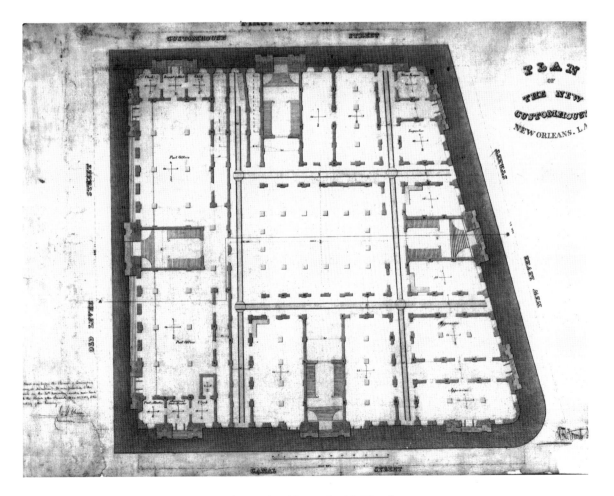

Design for the United States Custom House, New Orleans, by Alexander T. Wood, 1847–51. *National Archives, Washington*

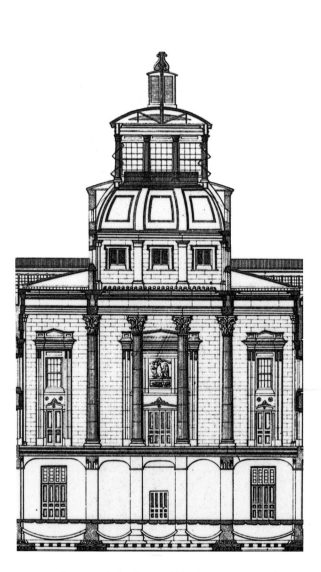

Sectional view of the General Business Room of the New Orleans Custom House, as conceived, from a lithograph, c. 1860. *Library of Congress*

Occupying more than two acres of ground, the Custom House was at the time of its construction the largest government building in the nation, except for the Capitol at Washington. To transport blocks of Massachusetts granite, weighing up to twenty tons each, temporary rail lines were laid from the levee to the site. Construction involved more than laying large granite blocks on top of each other: an intricate system of arches, iron braces, foundations, and lower brick walls four feet thick was required to support this tremendous structure. In February, 1854, Thomas Wharton, who continued as chief clerk of the works after serving briefly as supervising architect, toured the Custom House with friends: "They had no idea of its vast extent . . . until they saw the interior and its extensive and imposing system of groining. The Exterior work has been so long . . . encumbered with heavy scaffolding and unchanged in elevation, say 40 feet high, that it now fails to strike the passersby, and it is only when they see the busy hive within and ascend to the top of the second tier of groins that they realize the true magnitude and intricacy of the work." [42] In November, 1853, more than 160 men were at work. By March, 1854, construction had already consumed 10,886,942 bricks, 6,813 tons of granite, 3,875,721 feet of lumber and 1,056,381 pounds of iron for arches. [43] The weight of the building was so relentless that between 1851 and 1858, the Custom House settled nearly twenty-one inches.

Between 1853 and 1860, the supervising architect of the Custom House was Pierre G. T. Beauregard (1818–1893). Born in Louisiana, Beauregard graduated from West Point in 1838 and, after fighting under General Winfield Scott in Mexico, was stationed as an army engineer in New Orleans. In January, 1861, Beauregard served as superintendent of West Point for just four days before resigning his commission to return to the South. The first story of the Custom House was completed in 1856, and the collector of customs moved into improvised offices in July, 1856. By 1860 the walls were seventy-five feet high. Work at the Custom House was suspended between 1860 and 1871. The second story was completed in 1879, and the third story in 1881. The fourth story was never completed as planned, and the exterior cornice was simplified to make it more Classical in design as well as lighter in weight. The glory of the building is the General Business Room, even though the dome intended to rise above the hall's fifty-four-foot-high Corinthian columns was never built.

General Business Room, United States Custom House, Canal Street, New Orleans,
1848–81. *Library of Congress*

V. *Romantic Styles*

First Presbyterian Church, St. Charles Street, New Orleans, 1818–19, an early 19th-century French lithograph. The church also appears in a c. 1850 photograph on p. 113. *Historic New Orleans Collection*

In early 1818, a young minister from New England, the Reverend Sylvester Larned, came to New Orleans to lead a newly formed congregation of Presbyterians. Born at Pittsfield, Massachusetts, Larned had studied theology at Andover and Princeton. Benjamin Latrobe wrote that the young minister, whom he met in New Orleans, was both "Larned" by birth and "learned" by accomplishment.[1] Upon his arrival, Larned wrote: "It is contemplated to make the church of brick . . . about ninety feet by sixty. . . . Possibly the general plan of Dr. Mason's will be the model except that a church in this climate will need two additional doors in the side."[2] John Mitchell Mason, a prominent Presbyterian clergyman in New York, had built a church on Murray Street in 1812, a gable-roofed, two-story brick building with a spire rising above a slightly projecting center pavilion. The Presbyterian Church at New Orleans copied the general form of the church in New York but added Gothic details, the earliest example of the style in Louisiana. "They think of sending me to Philadelphia for an architect," Larned wrote.[3] In April, 1818, he was planning to proceed to New York to purchase half a million bricks and other materials.[4] The First Presbyterian Church on St. Charles Street was built in 1818–19 by William Brand. Later used by a group of Congregationalists led by the charismatic Dr. Theodore Clapp, the Church burned in 1851.

Because of its association with the great cathedrals of the Middle Ages, Gothic architecture was often the inspiration for ecclesiastical buildings, especially for Episcopalians and Catholics. In his *Essay on Gothic Architecture,* published in 1836, John Henry Hopkins, the Episcopal bishop of Vermont, described the transcendant association between Gothic design and Christian spirituality: "The multiple perpendicular lines of buttresses, crowned with pinnacles diminishing to a point, the mullioned windows, and the slender clustered pillars, lead the eye of the beholder upwards . . . in the sky . . . causing, by a kind of physical association, an impression of sublimity more exalted than any other sort of architecture can produce!"

James Dakin and his brother completed the design for St. Patrick's Church at 724 Camp Street in New Orleans in February, 1837. Their design featured a 185-foot-high tower, as tall as the great dome of the new St. Charles Hotel. Daringly, the architects eliminated the columns that traditionally supported the ceiling of a Gothic sanctuary. Instead, they provided a truss roof reinforced with the innovative use of cast-iron rods to create a ceiling seventy-three feet wide. In June, 1838, the Dakins contracted to build St. Patrick's. The cornerstone was laid in July, and, by the summer of the following year, the walls had risen two-thirds of their intended height.[5] Then, after an acrimonious dispute with the building committee over charges that the Dakins had not followed their own specifications, the architect-builders were discharged. The building committee then employed James Gallier, Sr., to complete the work. Gallier redesigned the altar and the apse behind it and added columns and fan-vaulting to the ceiling.[6] St. Patrick's was completed about 1841. Because of its tremendous width, modeled on the spacious proportions of neo-classical churches and facilitated by advanced engineering, the interior of St. Patrick's is one of the most cheerful of any Gothic churches in America. As we shall see, within ten years reformers would condemn cheerful churches like this, which merely embellished boxy buildings with Gothic frills instead of adopting the authentic proportions and expressive use of real materials found in medieval churches.

In March, 1837, Congress appropriated funds for construction of a United States Marine Hospital that was to be built outside New Orleans.[7] Designs were submitted by the Dakin brothers, Antonio Mondelli and his partner John Reynolds, the English-born W. L. Atkinson, the veteran builder Daniel H. Twogood, P. Brooks, a Mr. Shengerland, and Robert Mills. Mills (1781–1855) was born at Charleston, South Carolina, studied architecture with James Hoban, Thomas Jefferson, and Benjamin Latrobe and later described himself as the first native-born professionally trained architect in America. In 1836 Mills was appointed Federal Architect and in 1837 published model designs in the Greek and Gothic styles for marine hospitals that the government was planning to build in several ports. In December, 1837, Mills submitted his design for the Hospital at New Orleans, 200 feet long and 80 feet wide, two stories high over a raised basement, with a two-tiered colonnade flanked by square towers, battlemented walls, rear galleries, and a cupola. The basement would contain kitchens, dining rooms, storerooms, and baths; the first story would provide wards for the sick, an apothecary and offices; the second story, more wards for the sick; and the attic would contain a surgeon's hall and an anatomical laboratory.[8]

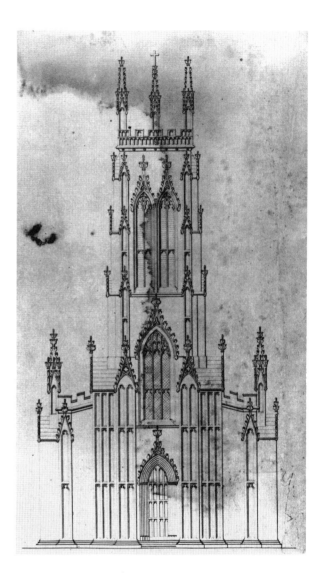

Design for St. Patrick's Church, New Orleans, by James Dakin and Charles Dakin, 1837. *New Orleans Public Library*

This page and opposite: Sectional views of St. Patrick's Church by James Dakin and Charles Dakin, 1837. *Louisiana State Museum (above), New Orleans Public Library (opposite)*

Revisions of design for St. Patrick's Church by James Gallier, Sr., 1839. *Louisiana State Museum*

St. Patrick's Church, 724 Camp Street, New Orleans, 1838–41.

Four pages from Robert Mills's diary in 1837, listing architects and builders who submitted proposals for the marine hospital at New Orleans, with sketches of the design by Mondelli and Reynolds and Mills's own ideas. *Manuscripts Division, Library of Congress*

Construction of the Marine Hospital began at McDonoughville, across the Mississippi River from New Orleans, in May, 1838. Perhaps in an attempt to economize, the builders Mondelli and Reynolds reduced the size of the building to 160 feet by 70 feet. Work was interrupted about 1841 by lack of funds, and the building was left a shell with a roof but few windows and no floors until 1845, when construction was resumed by the builder Joseph P. Clohecy, who had worked on the St. Charles Hotel and St. Patrick's Church. Completed in 1849, the Hospital was abandoned after less than a decade because of its swampy and inconvenient location. The Hospital, seized by Confederate troops who used the building to store powder, was destroyed by a mysterious explosion in December, 1861.

The Gothic design of the second Christ Church on Canal Street was provided by Thomas Kelah Wharton (1814–1862) in 1845. Born at Hull, England, Wharton sailed to America in 1830 to join his father who had established a farm in Ohio. Two years later, in May, 1832, Wharton returned to New York to work in the office of Martin Thompson, architect of the 1822–23 Second Bank of the United States and the 1827 Merchants Exchange and an early partner of Ithiel Town. Wharton lived in Thompson's household, where, he later recalled, he was "treated as one of themselves" by the family of that "truly worthy and kind-hearted man."[9] For several years, 1833–43, Wharton taught drawing at schools at Flushing, New York, William Augustus Mehlenburg's Institute and the Reverend Francis Hawks's St. Thomas Hall. When Hawks faced bankruptcy and moved to the South, Wharton followed the clergyman-schoolmaster to Holly Springs, Mississippi, where Hawks had established a new school. In 1844, Hawks was called to Christ Church, New Orleans, and asked Wharton to provide the design for a new building. Thus, Wharton recalled: "I gradually reverted back to the occupation in which I commenced life, architecture, which I was again led into from having made designs for Christ Church, New Orleans, during the last summer I spent in Holly Springs."[10] In early 1846, Wharton, having moved to New Orleans, was engaged in making detailed drawings, with suggestions from James Gallier, Sr., who was to be the builder. The contract for construction of the third Christ Church was signed in 1846; the building was completed in 1848 and abandoned in 1887.

Wharton spent the following eighteen months in 1846 and 1847 "pursuing closely my studies of architecture and executing some large drawings in perspective for Mr. Gallier."[11] In 1848 Wharton was appointed superintendent of construction of the New Orleans Custom House and worked under a succession of supervising architects throughout the 1850's. He

United States Marine Hospital, McDonoughville, 1838–49, a 19th-century lithograph. *Historic New Orleans Collection*

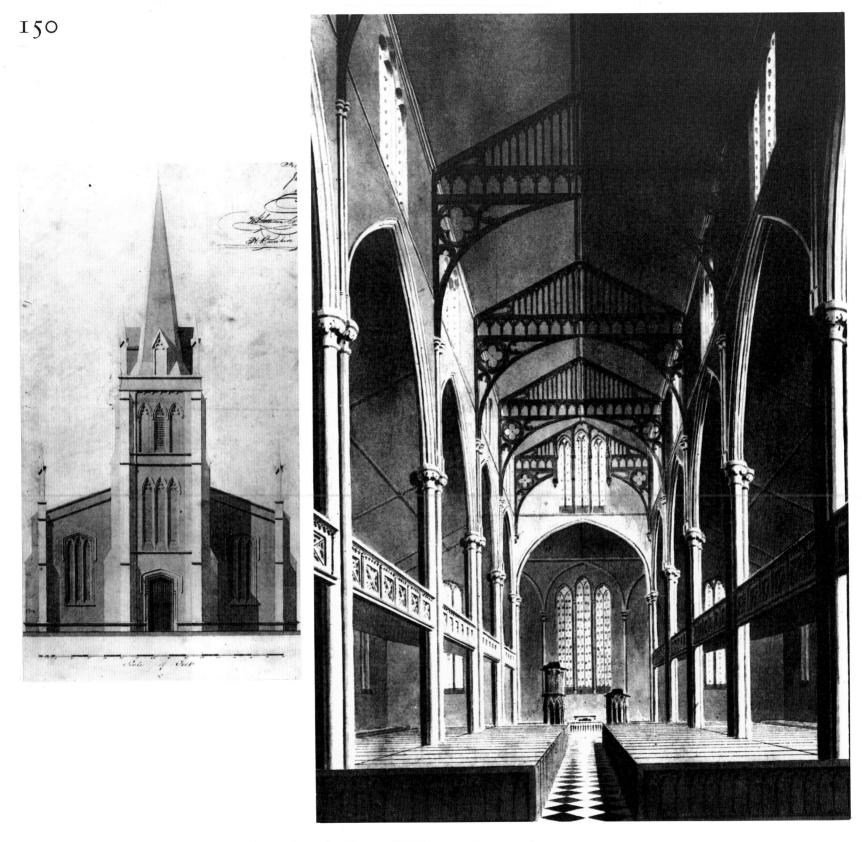

Christ Church, Canal Street, New Orleans, design by Thomas K. Wharton, 1844.
Historic New Orleans Collection

also continued to provide designs for private clients. Among those mentioned in Wharton's diary are the Steele Chapel, a Greek Ionic building erected for the Methodists on Felicity Street in 1850, the front of the German Methodist Church on Dryades Street in 1850, the Seamen's Home built in 1855 by the Kentucky-born William Day, a synagogue on St. Charles Street in 1855, a tower for the Baptist Church on Camp Street in 1855, a frame house for Mr. Reid on Apollo Street in 1856, a "small building for Mr. Cox" in 1856, plans for rebuilding the Seamen's Home in 1857, plans for a proposed hotel on Lafayette Square "150 × 150 and four stories high" in 1857, and warehouses on Fulton Street for the commission merchant William Whitehead in 1858.[12] Wharton died in 1862.

In the 1830's church reformers in England sought to revive the Anglican liturgy by modeling new buildings in the style of medieval parish churches. These simple, solemn buildings were intended to fuse function and symbolism by representing in wood and stone a holier, less secular, kind of religious life, the theology and traditions of the ancient church cleansed of 18th-century rationalism and Classicism. In place of the boxy, light-filled churches of the 18th and early 19th centuries, these buildings would be darker, narrower, more mysterious. The New York Ecclesiological Society, founded in 1848 by anglophile church leaders, advocated simple rather than elegant church design. The Society specified the use of real materials, wood and stone, instead of plaster and bricks, asymmetrical plans with projecting corner towers, provision for a separate chancel, and the use of comfortless benches rather than upholstered pews.

Christ Church, Napoleonville, despite its modest scale, is a significant example of Ecclesiology in the South, particularly because of its remote location. The architect was Frank Wills (1822–1856), who came from England to New York by way of Canada in 1847. He became one of the handful of architects endorsed by the Ecclesiologists, edited the Society's influential journal, and authored *Ancient Ecclesiological Architecture,* published at New York in 1850, in which he wrote: "As in morals, so in Architecture, honesty is the best policy. . . . Let us not be afraid of simplicity in building, and let us prefer a massive wall to a pretty moulding. . . . No house of God should be pretty!" In 1851 Wills formed a partnership with Henry Dudley (1813–1894), another Englishman with whom he had worked in Devonshire before coming to America. The vestrymen of Christ Church, Napoleonville, paid Wills $120 for plans in April, 1854, and the Church was built by George Ament in 1854–55.[13] A belfry and portico were added in 1896. Wills and Dudley also provided designs for two more conventional Gothic churches in Louisiana: St. Mary's, Tunica, 1857, and St. Stephen's, Innis, about 1858.

Christ Church, Canal Street, New Orleans, 1846–48, a 19th-century view. *Louisiana State Museum*

First Presbyterian Church, Lafayette Square, New Orleans, designed by Henry Howard and built by George Purves, a drawing by P. Gauldi, 1855. *First Presbyterian Church*

Gothic design was also employed to represent civic and academic virtue as well as spiritual authority. In January, 1846, James Dakin delivered his first proposal for the new United States Custom House at New Orleans. This design projected corner turrets, a crenellated parapet, a trefoil frieze, circular windows with inset quatrefoils, pointed windows, and heavy hood mouldings. The central room of the first story was intended to store goods as they passed through customs; the second story was to be the general business room of the customs; and the small rooms in the projecting corners were administrative offices. Perhaps the most arresting feature of Dakin's design was his innovative use of cast iron for structural columns as well as for Gothic embellishments. As we have already seen, though Dakin submitted two other, more conventional schemes for the Custom House (pages 136–138), the proposal of Alexander T. Wood, a Greek Revival design enlivened with Egyptian columns, was finally selected by the authorities.

Dakin redeveloped many of these Gothic ideas in late 1846 when he presented another Gothic design for a new Capitol to be built at Baton Rouge, a town on the east bank of the Mississippi eighty miles above New Orleans, which had been designated the new seat of government. When Dakin delivered his design in January, 1847, he advocated the use of the Gothic style because its details could be executed economically in cast iron and because it would be a novel style: "A Design in the Grecian or Roman order of Architecture . . . would unavoidably appear to be a mere copy of some other Edifice already erected and often repeated in every City and Town of our Country."[14] In May, the authorities approved Dakin's plan, and construction commenced the following month. Cast-iron window frames, sills, tracery, battlement caps, quatrefoil panels, cornice, clustered columns, and stringcourses—350,000 pounds of cast iron—would be supplied by the Pittsburgh firm of Knap and Totten. In July, 1847, on his way to confer with the foundry in Pittsburgh, Dakin traveled on a steamboat up the Mississippi. At Cincinnati, another passenger attempted to steal the working drawings for the Capitol, but Dakin's son spotted the thief before he could escape.

In October, 1847, Dakin began laying out trenches for the foundations of the Capitol at Baton Rouge. There were frustrating delays with slow shipments of bricks and cast iron. In May, 1848, Maunsell White, chairman of the building committee, advised Dakin: "Keep cool or you will make me too hot to be handled!"[15] In July, Dakin and the chief mason, William Pratt, had a fist fight in front of scores of workmen at the construction site. Dakin recalled: "I had during the morning been employed in throwing from the stagings a large quantity of soft and very bad bricks,

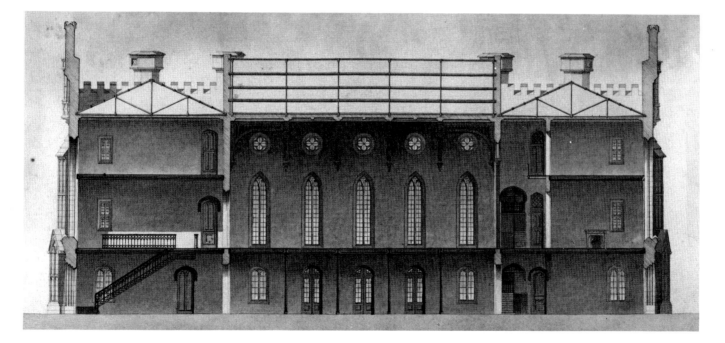

This page and opposite: First design for the United States Custom House, New Orleans, by James Dakin, 1846. *New Orleans Public Library*

Louisiana State Capitol, Baton Rouge, 1847–50, rebuilt within its standing walls
in 1880–82.

and had also thrown over some portions of walls which had been built with . . . bad bricks. In the midst of which occupation, Mr. Pratt came suddenly up to me in a hostile attitude and at the same time using menacing words and expressions at which I became enraged and struck at Pratt. A general contest then commenced and blows were passed. . . . The Mayor of Baton Rouge had us both arrested for disorderly conduct." [16] In September, 1848, Alexander Mathers, Dakin's chief assistant at the Capitol, died of yellow fever. In June, 1849, Dakin dismissed a slater named Michael Kenny, a thirty-nine-year-old Irishman, described by the architect as "a drunken vagabond." [17] The Capitol was completed in 1850.

The novel design of the Capitol's interior provoked the consternation of an 1852 visitor: "You enter either Chamber—they both represent the same follies. All around and above you, common timber has been tortured into oak of the most excessive color and remarkable grain. Above, it impersonates giant beams, which pretend to support the whole superstructure. This same oak is dug out into little troughs, with ornamented prows nailed to the walls, while the arch over the Speaker's chair mingles with its oak specimens of the Chinese painter's pencil. The smaller appropriations of this oak comprise curious little contrivances which seem to have been cut out of cake moulds. Imagine that eight or ten columns of wood, some fluted and some square, and some any way, all of different sizes and lengths, and that they had, by some sudden freak, been thrown confusedly together with a great deal of other stuff—that you then put two little boys on it, one with a hatchet and auger, the other with a saw and foot adze, and let them work away at it for about a week—then get all the muddy, yellow and sickly green paint you can find; mix some lampblack, white lead and Spanish brown, and throw it on with buckets. When it is just dry enough to be sticky and catch lint, you have a picture of the Speaker's seat!" [18] The interior was lost in 1862, when the Capitol burned. The Capitol was rebuilt within its standing walls in 1880–82 by New Orleans-born William A. Freret, who added a skylighted rotunda and eight cast-iron Moorish turrets, subsequently removed.

In 1850 the builder George Purves designed six brick stores at 325-343 Carondelet Street in New Orleans. Built by Thomas Murray, they featured drip mouldings over the upper windows. James Dakin projected a similar building, a drawing of which survives among the architect's papers at the New Orleans Public Library. In 1851–52, James Gallier, Jr., designed a Gothic railroad station at Carrollton, a suburban resort with pleasure gardens and a many-galleried hotel four miles upriver from New Orleans. This whimsical building was demolished about 1891. Gallier, Jr., also designed a Gothic-front office with cast-iron clustered col-

Design for an unidentified Gothic commercial building, New Orleans, by James Dakin. *New Orleans Public Library*

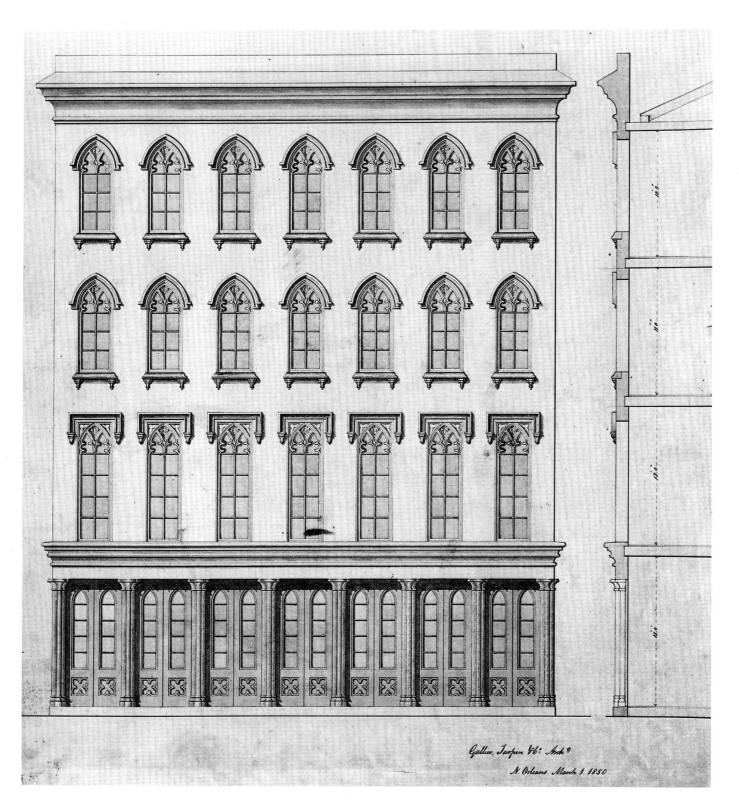

One of three surviving drawings for the Leeds and Company Store, New Orleans, by Gallier, Turpin and Company, March, 1850. *Labrot Collection, Southeastern Architectural Archive, Tulane University Library, Gift of Sylvester Labrot*

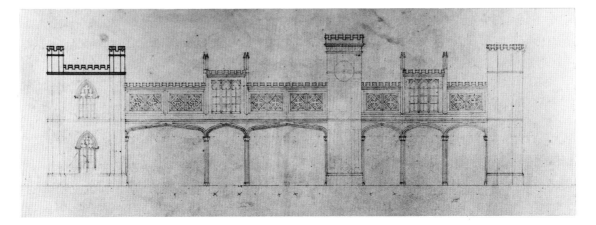

Railroad Station, Carrollton, 1851, two elevations by James Gallier, Jr., and a
19th-century photograph. *Drawings from Historic New Orleans Collection,
photograph from Louisiana State Museum*

Asylum for the Deaf and Dumb, Baton Rouge, 1852, a perspective view by Adrien Persac and a 19th-century photograph. *Painting from Anglo-American Art Museum, Louisiana State University, Baton Rouge; photograph from Suydam Collection, Louisiana State University Library, Baton Rouge*

Orange Grove, Thomas Asheton Morgan House, Braithwaite vicinity, design by
William L. Johnston, c. 1847. *Louisiana State Museum*

umns, drip mouldings, and trefoils set in pointed windows for the iron manufacturer Leeds and Company. The Leeds and Company store at 923 Tchoupitoulas Street was built in 1852, but the earliest of three Gallier drawings for it is dated 1850. In 1852, an otherwise unknown J. S. Brown designed a Gothic-style Asylum for the Deaf and Dumb at Baton Rouge, one-half mile downriver from James Dakin's Capitol. Used for many years by Louisiana State University, the old Asylum was destroyed in 1947. Probably the most surprising use of Gothic architecture was for a livery stable on Perdido Street in New Orleans, designed in 1853 by Francis D. Gott, a forty-three-year-old builder from New York. "The style of this horse palace will be of the first order of pointed architecture, Saxon Anglo [sic], Norman, Gothic—a composite."[19] In 1854 the veteran builder George Purves designed a Gothic courthouse for St. Charles Parish at Hahnville. Its builders were Robert Sittle and Peter Middlemiss.[20] The contracts for the stable and courthouse have survived, but there are no drawings or photographs of these intriguing Gothic buildings.

In the South generally but in Louisiana particularly, builders were not attracted to the Gothic style for houses. The carving and casting of its complicated ornament were more expensive than relatively simple Greek columns, while Italian villas, with shady loggias, seemed better suited to the climate. Significantly, the earliest documented Gothic house in Louisiana was Orange Grove, built in 1847–49 near Braithwaite, Plaquemines Parish, on the east bank of the Mississippi, for Thomas Asheton Morgan, an absentee cotton planter who spent most of the year in Philadelphia.[21] Morgan's architect was William L. Johnston (1811–1849) of Philadelphia, who taught architectural drawing between 1839 and 1845 and contributed designs to the 14th edition of Peter Nicholson's *Carpenter's New Guide,* which would appear at Philadelphia in 1850.[22] Johnston's drawings for the house at Orange Grove, which he prepared at Philadelphia, featured steep gables with decorated bargeboards, tall clustered chimneystacks, heavy hood mouldings, and trellised verandahs. The house at Orange Grove, already reduced to a ruin, burned in 1982.

James Dakin, with his demonstrated knack with Gothic design, may have had a hand in two other rare domestic essays in that style. In January, 1849, Maunsell White, chairman of the building committee of the State Capitol, thanked the architect for drawings for a "villa *à la mode Gothique.*"[23] The drawings have been lost, and there is no record that this house was ever built. Nearly as mysterious was Afton Villa, the home of David Barrow, the wealthiest planter in West Feliciana Parish, descended from the distinguished North Carolina family who had come to Louisiana during the territorial period. About 1849 Barrow decided to

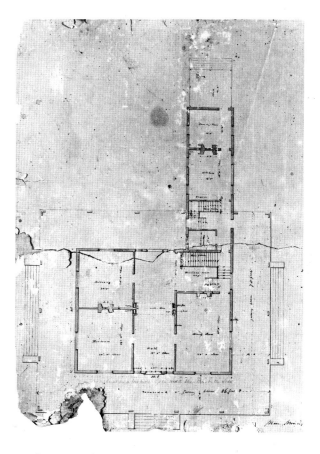

William L. Johnston's plan of Orange Grove. *Louisiana State Museum*

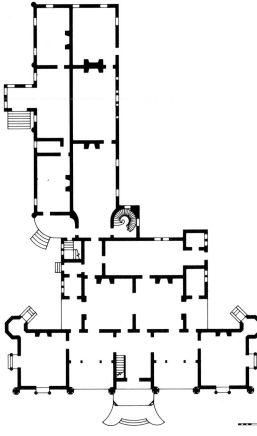

Afton Villa, David Barrow House, West Feliciana Parish, c. 1850. *Library of Congress*

View of the porches and entrance passage at Afton Villa. *Library of Congress*

enlarge his old house to satisfy the requirements of a new wife. Located just thirty miles from Baton Rouge, Afton Villa owed its new Gothic styling either to James Dakin individually or the influence of his conspicuous new Capitol. We might also speculate that Maunsell White passed on Dakin's drawings for a "villa *à la mode Gothique*" to his friend David Barrow. The interior featured a walnut stair carved with quatrefoils and walls painted to resemble Sienna marble, with other details imitating lapis lazuli, red basalt, and Egyptian marble.[24] Afton Villa's rather whacky exterior, with second-story porches and recessed terraces covered by a gigantic series of intersecting pointed arches supported by clustered columns or terminating in pendants, is best understood as an attempt to adapt Gothic design to the traditional Louisiana plantation house. Afton Villa burned in 1963—probably with any documentation of the architect and construction.

Books had long been important for the spread of architectural styles. Books of the 18th and early 19th centuries had been illustrated dictionaries, containing pictures of the Classical orders, details of capitals, columns, and entablatures, with solutions to geometrical problems relating to the construction of stairs, walls, and roofs, selected designs for doors, windows, chimneypieces, and mouldings, and a few elevations and plans for sample houses and churches. By the mid-19th century, authors and publishers had begun to create more elaborate books to serve the needs of an expanding profession. These larger and more comprehensive works featured details, plans, perspective views, and interior details for many model buildings in many styles—Greek, Italian, Swiss, and even Oriental—often with specific suggestions for landscaping, painting, furnishings, cost estimates, and even philosophical essays on style.

One of the most popular mid-century pattern books was William H. Ranlett's *The Architect,* published at New York in 1847–49. Two designs from that work were probably the inspiration for a striking Gothic house built on the outskirts of New Orleans in 1849–50 for Nathaniel Wilkinson, a Virginia-born banker, at 1015 South Carrollton Avenue. Ranlett's Design X appears to have suggested the cruciform plan and his Design V provided Gothic details for the leaded casements, decorated bargeboards, and porches.

The most popular of all mid-century pattern books was *The Architecture of Country Houses,* published at New York in 1850, by the New York horticulturist and architectural theorist Andrew Jackson Downing. Downing was not himself an architect and published designs provided by others, especially Alexander Jackson Davis (1803–1892) of New York City. Design XXIII of *The Architecture of Country Houses,* a small

Design X of William H. Ranlett's *The Architect* (New York, 1847–49), a probable model for Nathaniel Wilkinson's cruciform house in New Orleans, 1849–50. *Private Collection*

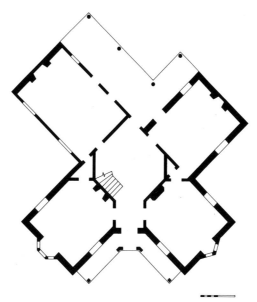

Nathaniel Wilkinson House, 1015 South Carrollton Avenue, New Orleans,
1849–50. *Southeastern Architectural Archive, Tulane University Library*

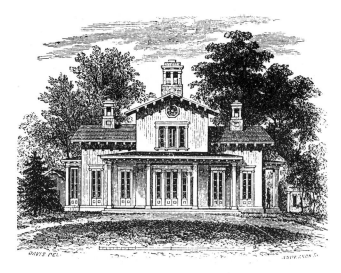

Albert Heaton House, Franklin vicinity, 1853, with its model, Design XXIII of
A. J. Downing's *The Architecture of Country Houses* (New York, 1850). *Downing
book in private collection*

board-and-batten villa designed by Davis for L. B. Brown of Rahway, New Jersey, became the model for a similar cottage built in 1853 for New England-born Albert Heaton outside Franklin, Louisiana. So delightful, convenient, and practical, this design was also reproduced in North Carolina and Mississippi. Thus, a house at Rahway, New Jersey, spawned architectural offspring in three Southern states!

About 1850 James Gallier, Sr., had turned over his architectural office to his son. Born at Huntingdon, England, in 1827, where his father was building a prison, James Gallier, Jr., was brought to America in 1832 and spent most of his youth in New York City with his mother, who could never endure the ennervating climate of Louisiana, and his Uncle John, a designer and manufacturer of plaster ornaments. James, Jr., was educated at Francis Hawks's school on Long Island, where Thomas Wharton was teacher of art, and at the University of North Carolina, from which he was graduated in 1845. The younger Gallier was assisted for several years in the office by John Turpin (1810–1876), an English-born bookkeeper who had worked for Gallier, Sr., and remained in the office until the spring of 1858, when he returned to his earlier career as a wine merchant. Gallier, Jr., was also assisted by Richard Esterbrook (1813–1906), another Englishman who had worked for the elder Gallier as a stair-builder and foreman of construction.

At a time when few architects had an opportunity to see the great buildings of the world, James Gallier, Jr., benefitted from several years of travel in Europe with his father in the late 1840's. Though a careful survey of building contracts indicates that much of Gallier's work was devoted to the design and construction of utilitarian stores and warehouses, the best of his residential work reflects the informed self-confidence of a world traveler. The Leeds and Company office, designed about 1850–52, and the Carrollton Railway Station, 1851, were Gothic designs that signaled new departures for the Gallier office.

In 1854, Gallier and Turpin produced drawings of a villa for Horace Cammack, a cotton merchant for whom Gallier had designed and built brick stores on Carondelet Street in 1850 and 1851. The tall tower, wide bracketed eaves, round-headed casement windows, and irregular massing were a daring surprise, for Louisiana builders generally shunned the Italian Villa style. Elsewhere in the South, it became the most popular Romantic style, because Italianate buildings were easier to build than Gothic buildings, and because the wide, overhanging eaves and long casement windows and shady loggias of Italian villas seemed better suited to the Southern climate. The two most important examples in Louisiana were two demolished villas, Sherwood and Gossypia, built in remote East

Horace Cammack Villa, New Orleans, design by James Gallier, Jr., and John Turpin, 1854. *Historic New Orleans Collection*

Edmund J. Forstall House, St. Louis Street, New Orleans, design by James Gallier, Jr., and John Turpin, 1854. *Historic New Orleans Collection*

Carroll Parish in the late 1850's, probably by a builder who had come downriver from Memphis or St. Louis.[25]

In the same year, 1854, Gallier and Turpin projected an Italianate house for another cotton merchant, Edmund J. Forstall, at 920 St. Louis Street. Its distinctive design—the rusticated first story with round-headed windows set into arches, the *piano nobile* with cast-iron balcony and tall windows, and the elongated proportions emphasized with tall Corinthian pilasters—may have been inspired by an unlikely source, Robert Adam's 1772 design for the William Wynn House, St. James's Square, London, as illustrated in Adam's *Works in Architecture,* published in 1778.

In December, 1854, the Mechanics Institute, devoted to the charitable and educational activities of craftsmen and artists in New Orleans, burned. The design for a new building was promptly provided by James Gallier, Jr.[26] Like Edmund Forstall's house of 1854, the Institute featured a rusticated ground story, a *piano nobile,* and an attic, supported by Corinthian pilasters, rising above the cornice. *The Daily Picayune* described the interior arrangements of the Institute: "On the first story the library room is to be located, together with the mechanics' lecture room, the itinerant lecture room, the cabinet of natural history, and a large vestibule with spacious staircases. The library room is 75 feet long, 36 feet wide, and 16 feet high. . . . On the next story is the main lecture room, which is to be 100 feet long, 72 feet broad, and 30 feet high . . . to be finished in a very beautiful style with pilasters and rich panel work. . . . On the same floor are to be two large retiring rooms. The principal room in the third story is 90 feet long by 30 feet wide . . . designed as a cabinet for the reception of models and inventions. The fourth story is cut up into classrooms."[27] The Mechanics Institute was demolished in 1908.

In January and February, 1857, James Gallier, Jr., was working on drawings for a three-story brick house to be built at the corner of Canal and Marais streets for Michael Heine, another cotton broker for whom Gallier built stores on Common Street in 1850, Carondelet Street in 1851, and Canal Street in 1857.[28] Gallier took special pains to provide delightful and convenient arrangements for the interior: double parlors divided by a double screen of columns with folding doors that could be closed for family evenings or hidden in wall pockets for parties; a cheerful octagonal dining room that projects into the garden; and a separate stair and passage for servants. In the same year, 1857, Gallier produced a similar, though more modest, design for his own house, which was completed in the fall of 1858 at 1132 Royal Street. Splendidly restored in the 1970's, Gallier House is open to the public.

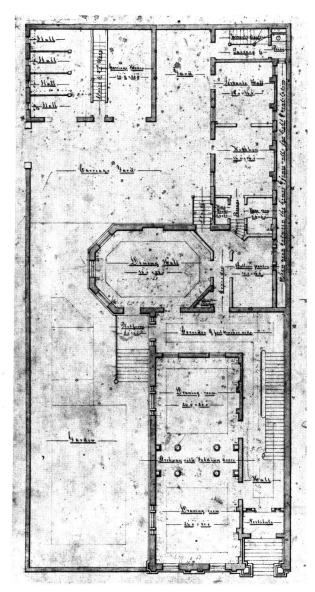

Plan of Michael Heine House, Canal Street, New Orleans, by James Gallier, Jr., and John Turpin, 1857. *Labrot Collection, Southeastern Architectural Archive, Tulane University Library, Gift of Sylvester Labrot*

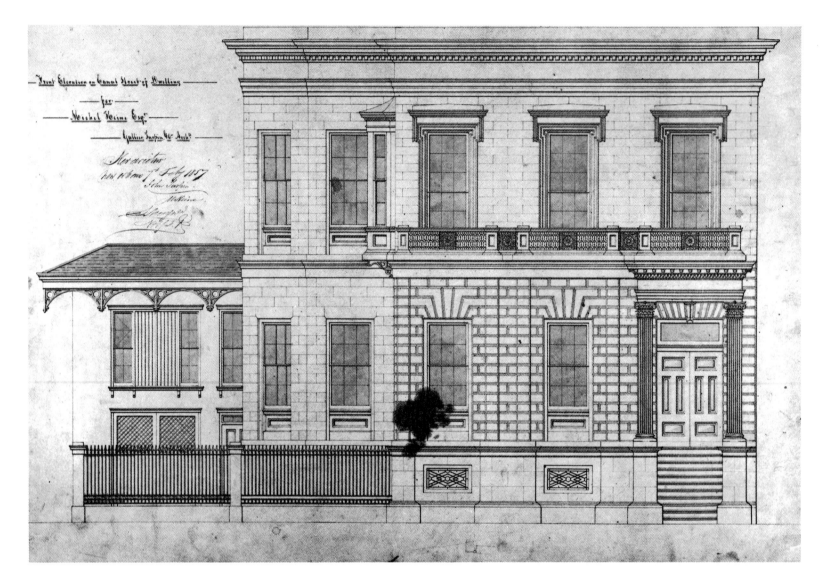

Michael Heine House, New Orleans, elevation drawing by Gallier, Turpin and Company, 1857. *Labrot Collection, Southeastern Architectural Archive, Tulane University Library, Gift of Sylvester Labrot*

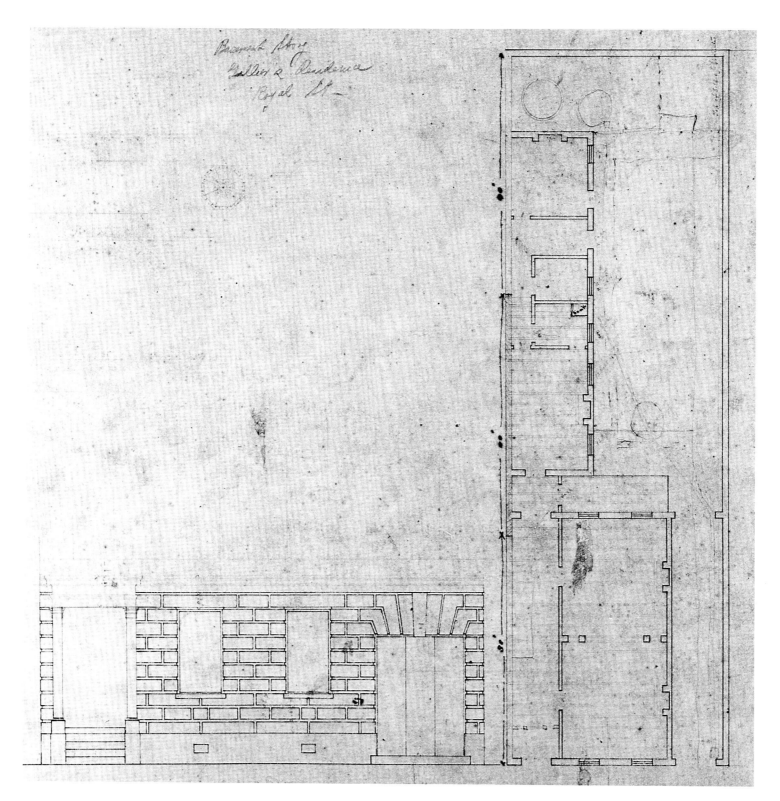

Study for James Gallier, Jr., House, drawn by the architect, 1857. *Labrot Collection, Southeastern Architectural Archive, Tulane University Library, Gift of Sylvester Labrot*

James Gallier, Jr., House, 1132 Royal Street, New Orleans, 1857–58. *Gallier House, Tulane University*

James Gallier, Jr., House, view of parlors.

In early 1859, Gallier prepared designs for Charles Boudousquié, manager of opera productions at the Orleans Theater, who had decided to establish a new opera house in New Orleans. Construction began at the corner of Bourbon and Toulouse streets in the spring of 1859. To hasten construction, so the theater could open in time for the fall musical season, bonfires were lit in the streets to permit laborers to work all night. In September, 1859, as it was nearing completion, the architect Thomas K. Wharton surveyed the exterior of the Opera House: "Sorry to remark the usual effect of hasty building—evidence of unequal subsidence—bad brickwork—immense mortar joints—cracks everywhere—and the construction, though bad, was no worse than the design and details of the exterior which are simply abominable."[29] The design, with its one-story portico surmounted by engaged columns and pilasters, rusticated first story and round ends, recalls the Mechanics Institute Hall produced by Gallier in 1856.

The Opera House was completed in eight short months and opened in December, 1859. The auditorium was ninety feet wide and fifty-six feet high, with four tiers of boxes and seats for 1,600 spectators. The proscenium arch was supported by four fluted Corinthian columns, two on each side of the stage, with three tiers of proscenium boxes. "The whole house is painted white, and the decorations on the fronts of the boxes are in gold, the first circle with rich festoons, and those above it with panel work. A magnificent mirror in a gold frame, on the wall on each side of the proscenium, adds greatly to the picturesque effect of the auditorium."[30] The Opera House burned in 1919.

About 1861 Gallier and Esterbrook designed a massive Italian villa in a parklike setting near Esplanade Avenue for the cotton merchant Florence A. Luling. The design, so exquisitely delineated by the architects, featured rustication, quoins, impost stripes, and Palladian doorways, a terrace and bridges leading to flanking dependencies. The Luling villa survives, though divided into apartments, its flankers demolished and its park diminished. James Gallier, Jr., died in 1868.

Another design for the Opera House had been submitted by J. N. B. dePouilly. Magnificent though dePouilly's plan was, with its array of arches, pilasters, and statues, it was not chosen, for the authorities could not have forgotten that the galleries of the Orleans Theater, designed by dePouilly, had collapsed in 1854. His reputation tarnished, dePouilly began teaching "linear drawing applied to buildings, machinery, surveying, with landscapes and perspective" in 1854. In July, 1857, he announced the future publication of *Home Illustrations*, views of dwellings, plantations, public buildings, churches, monuments, and landscape in Louisi-

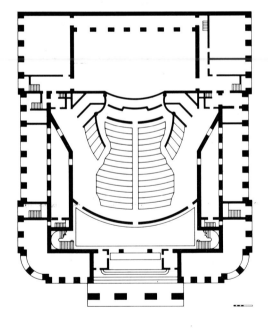

Opera House, New Orleans, 1859, painting by Adrien Persac and plan of the principal story. *Persac painting from Historic New Orleans Collection*

Opera House, Bourbon Street, New Orleans, 1859, a photograph about 1900.
Louisiana State University Library, Baton Rouge

Florence A. Luling Villa, 1436 Leda Court, New Orleans, c. 1861, design by James Gallier, Jr., and Richard Esterbrook, with an early photograph. *Elevation from Labrot Collection, Southeastern Architectural Archive, Tulane University Library, Gift of Sylvester Labrot; photograph from Louisiana State University Library, Baton Rouge.*

ana, each issue to include "a painting in water colors, and a fine lead pencil drawing or a fine sepia painting, with historical or descriptive notices, on fine white drawing paper, large quarto size."[31] Alas, there is no record that this work was ever published, and in his last years, dePouilly supported himself by working in the city surveyor's office.

While commissions like the Opera House went to other architects, dePouilly poured his creative energies into fantasy buildings in at least three volumes of sketchbooks. In the one surviving sketchbook, dePouilly displays the erudition, originality, and wit of a gifted designer, playfully creating various façades for a single plan in different styles—Greek, Roman, Gothic, Moorish, or French Renaissance. A proposed mansion for Pierre Soulé, a French-born, Paris-trained lawyer and diplomat, received a Greek and French Renaissance exterior. A proposed house for Cyprien Dufour, another attorney who had read law in Pierre Soulé's office, received a Greek and a Palladian exterior. Dufour's house was finally designed, not by dePouilly, but by Henry Howard in 1858. In 1860, dePouilly was preoccupied with alternate schemes for a house to be built at the corner of Esplanade Avenue and the Bayou Road. This unusual triangular site inspired the architect to consider several highly original plans and exterior styles, including a Swiss chalet. Like many of the projects in the sketchbook, there is no record that any of these designs was ever executed. DePouilly died at New Orleans in 1875.

Despite the region's reputed antipathy to industry, prefabrication had a long and honorable history in Southern architecture. James Dakin had pioneered the use of cast iron in Louisiana, erecting large cast-iron verandahs across the street fronts of a New Orleans hotel in 1836, reinforcing the ceiling of St. Patrick's Church with cast-iron rods in 1838, and ordering 350,000 pounds of cast iron for the State Capitol at Baton Rouge in 1847. Charles Leeds, the Connecticut-born proprietor of an iron foundry in New Orleans for whom James Gallier, Jr., designed a Gothic-style building with cast-iron clustered columns and drip mouldings, became an early mayor of the city.

In the late 1840's, manufacturers discovered that cast iron was stronger, lighter, and cheaper than masonry construction and that it also allowed more light and ventilation to enter within a building. Cast-iron capitals for the second St. Charles Hotel came from J. L. Jackson of Brooklyn, New York, in 1852.[32] Daniel Badger, the Massachusetts-born manufacturer of cast iron in New York (who had worked for three years, 1818–21, as a jewelry engraver at Savannah, Georgia), produced store fronts in New Orleans for J. B. Lee and Paul Tulane. The façade of the Tulane Building on Camp Street in New Orleans was identical to Cary's Building

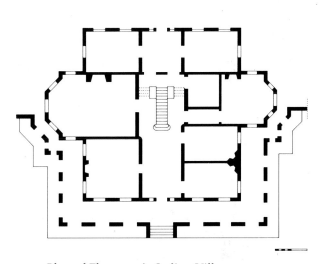

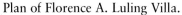

Plan of Florence A. Luling Villa.

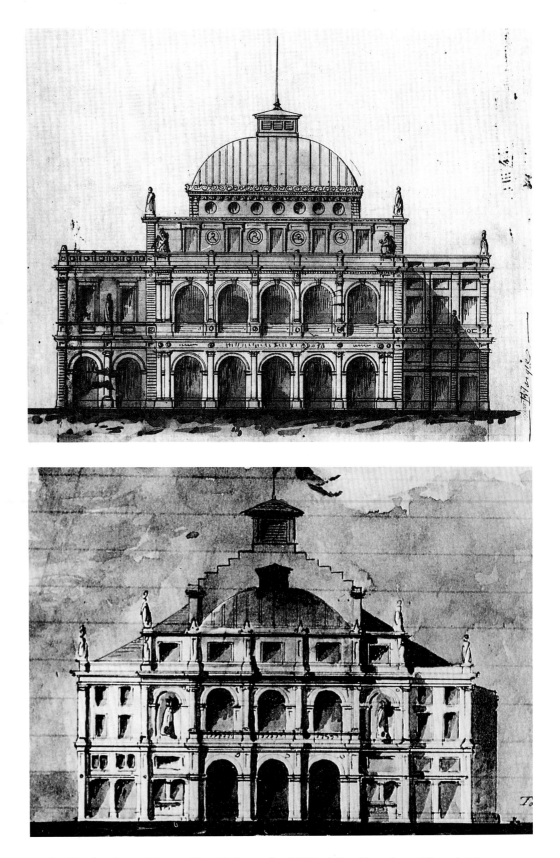

Studies for Opera House, New Orleans, by J.N.B. dePouilly, 1859. *Historic New Orleans Collection*

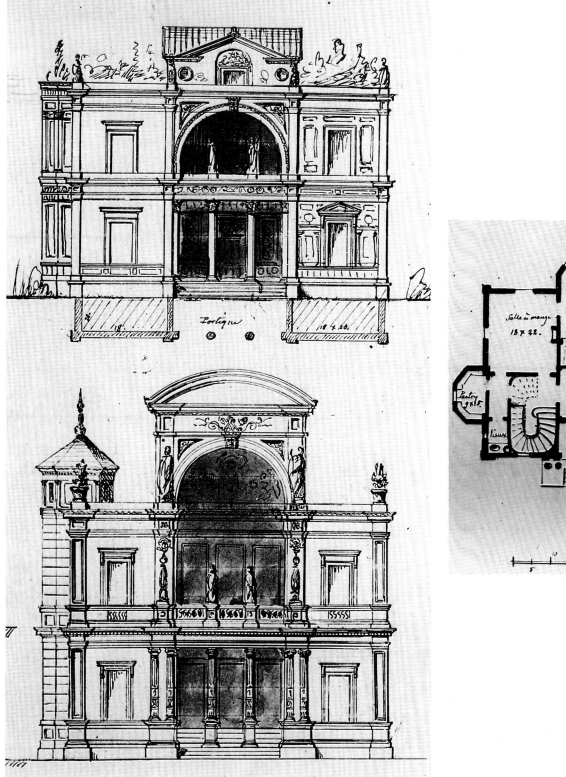

Studies for an unidentified house, New Orleans, by J.N.B. dePouilly, c. 1859. *Historic New Orleans Collection*

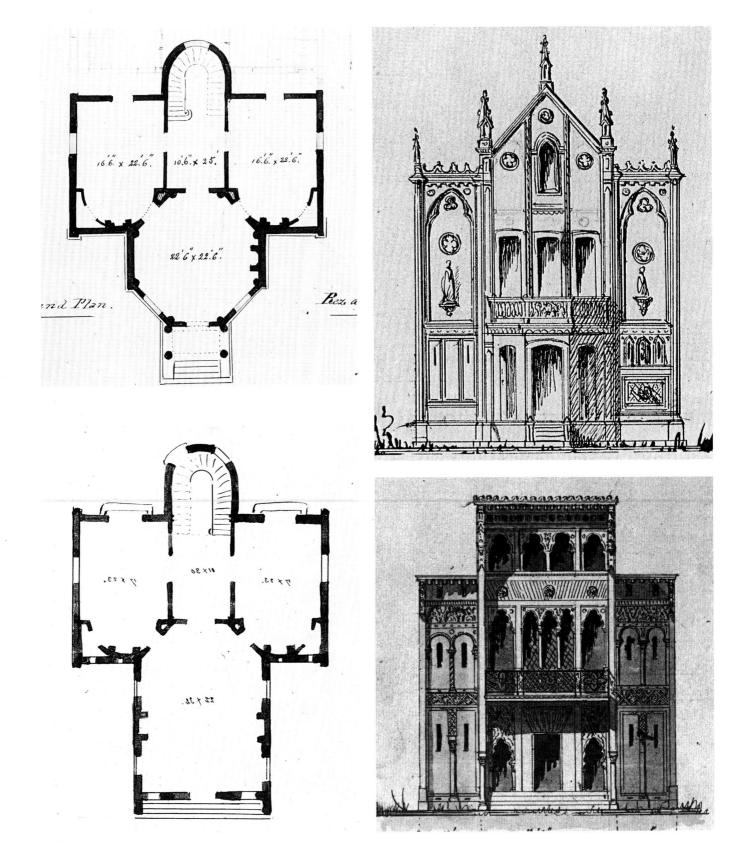

Gothic and Moorish studies for an unidentified house, New Orleans, by J.N.B.
dePouilly, c. 1860. *Historic New Orleans Collection*

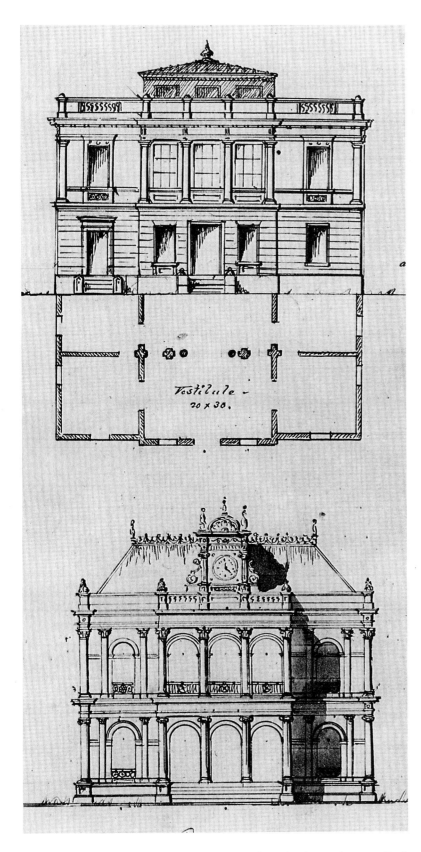

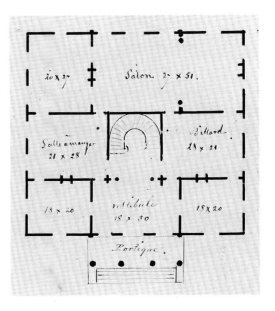

·Greek and Roman studies for a house for Charles Dufour on Esplanade Avenue, New Orleans, by J.N.B. dePouilly, c. 1858. *Historic New Orleans Collection*

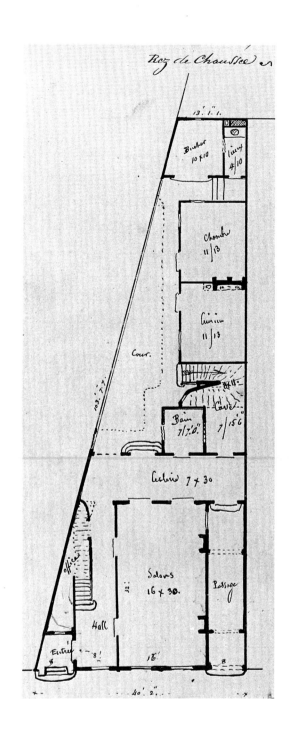

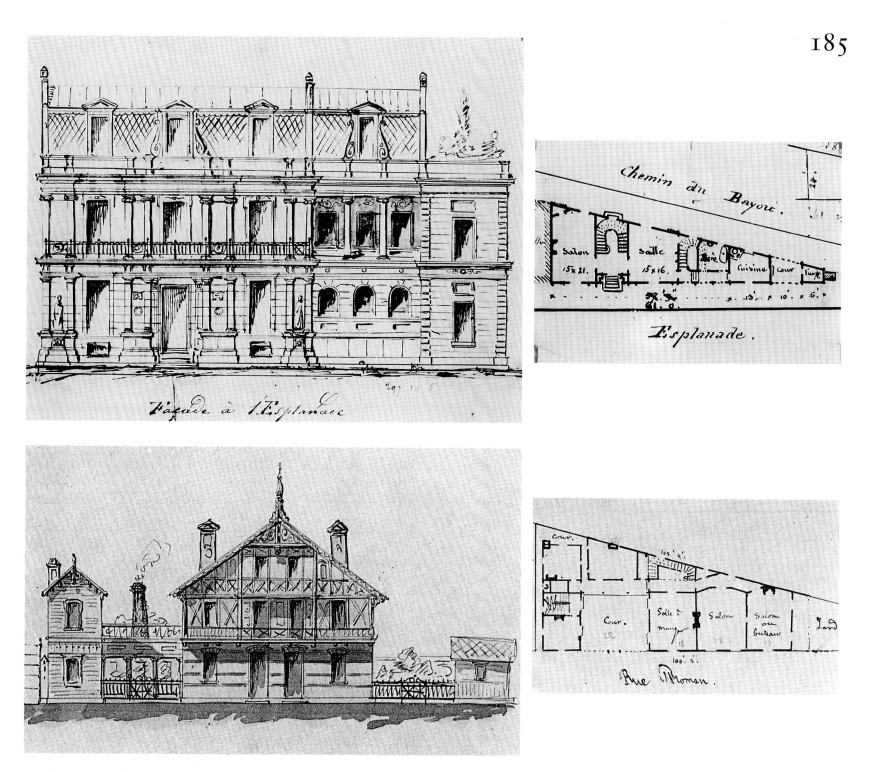

This page and opposite: Greek, French Renaissance, Palladian, and Swiss studies for a house to be built on a triangular site on Esplanade Avenue, New Orleans, by J. N. B. dePouilly, c. 1860. *Historic New Orleans Collection*

Design for cast-iron front of Theodore Frois and Company Office, Canal Street, New Orleans, by W.A. Freret, 1859. *Louisiana State Museum*

on Chambers Street in New York City. Daniel Badger also provided cast iron for the second Marine Hospital at New Orleans in 1856–60. In 1859 Louis E. Reynolds erected a store on Camp and Common streets with a cast-iron front shipped to New Orleans from Trenton, New Jersey. This store was designed by Stephen D. Button of Philadelphia, architect of buildings at Savannah and Columbus, Georgia, and Montgomery, Alabama.[33]

In September, 1854, the New Orleans architect Thomas K. Wharton viewed the new cast-iron façade of Benjamin Florance's office at the corner of Natchez and Camp streets with mingled admiration and skepticism: "The iron is all put together . . . and it is *all* iron. . . . These fronts are a great improvement in store building, but I fear will give rise to an incalculable amount of false ornamentation. The facility with which ornaments are executed in such a plastic material is a temptation too strong to introduce them every where until the great principle in architecture is soon lost sight of—that construction is but a means to an end . . . but where the end is not palpable the ornament becomes contemptible!"[34]

One wonders what Wharton thought of the Moresque Building, a cast-iron confection begun in 1859 on Camp and Poydras streets, facing Lafayette Square, for J. C. Barelli, an Italian-born merchant, in a melange of styles described at the time as "Islamic, Arabic, Sarcenic, Hindo revival." The architect was William Alfred Freret (1833–1911). The son of an architect named William Freret (1804–1864), young William studied briefly with James Gallier, Sr., and designed the 1856 synagogue on Carondelet Street and the 1859 Touro Almshouse. The Moresque Building was completed in 1865 by James Freret, the architect's cousin, who had worked for George Purves in 1856 and for William Alfred Freret in 1857–60. William Alfred Freret was state engineer of Louisiana in 1866–68, restored the Capitol at Baton Rouge in the 1880's, and served as supervising architect of the U.S. Treasury in 1887–89. The Moresque Building burned in 1897. William A. Freret also designed the cast-iron front of the Theodore Frois store on Canal Street, built in 1859 and now demolished.

Thus, the slow, but relentless and accelerating, process of cultural change, which had begun with settlers coming to New Orleans and northern and eastern Louisiana, was facilitated by mass production. Imminently, the Civil War would bring a further challenge to Louisiana's distinctive traditions and lead to the triumph of nationalism and industrialization.

Moresque Building, Lafayette Square, New Orleans, 1859–61, a late-19th-century
photograph. *Louisiana State Museum*

Notes

The author is tremendously grateful, for generous help, suggestions, and information, to Barbara Sorelle Bacot, Division of Historic Preservation, Louisiana Department of Culture, Recreation, and Tourism; Faye Phillips, Louisiana State University Library, Baton Rouge; Samuel Wilson, Jr., scholar-architect of New Orleans; and Walter F. Wolfe, III, Historic New Orleans Collection.

The place to begin studying Louisiana architecture is the Louisiana Division of Historic Preservation, Department of Culture, Recreation, and Tourism, in Baton Rouge, which maintains files of historic buildings throughout the state. These files are a handy guide to important buildings, with information about their history and clues for further research. The following footnotes, in lieu of a separate bibliography, acknowledge the author's debt to other scholars.

I. THE COLONY

1. Samuel Wilson, Jr., *Vieux Carré, Its Plan, Its Growth, Its Architecture* (New Orleans, 1968), 9. Throughout this chapter, the author is indebted to Samuel Wilson, Jr., *The Architecture of Colonial Louisiana* (Lafayette, Louisiana, 1987), a collection of his many articles on the subject.

2. Charles E. O'Neill, *Charlevoix's Louisiana* (Baton Rouge, 1977), 273–274.

3. Wilson, "An Architectural History of the Royal Hospital and the Ursuline Convent of New Orleans" in *The Architecture of Colonial Louisiana*, 161–220.

4. *Ibid.*, 121.

5. Dunbar Rowland and Albert Godfrey Sanders, *Mississippi Provincial Archives*, II (Jackson, 1929), 440–442. In February, 1725, the authorities in Louisiana reported: "The large warehouse is completely finished with the exception of the stairs. The house of the Reverend Capuchin Fathers is erected and the framework complete. The contractors of the lumber for the church are delivering it at present. The lodging that has been intended for the Officers is going to serve as the church until the one on which work is being done is finished and we have not yet thought of making a pavilion for lodging the employees." *Ibid.*, 408.

6. *Ibid.*, 489, 510–511.

7. Wilson, *Colonial Louisiana*, 124.

8. *Ibid.*, 128.

9. Gabriel Gravier and Olivia Blanchard, Jr., "Voyage of the Ursuline Nuns to New Orleans," Survey of Federal Archives in Louisiana, typescript, 1940, 63.

10. Rowland and Sanders, *Mississippi Provincial Archives*, II, 631.

11. Rowland and Sanders, *Mississippi Provincial Archives*, I (Jackson, 1927), 127.

12. Henry P. Dart, "The Career of Dubreuil in French Louisiana," *Louisiana Historical Quarterly* (hereafter cited as *LHQ*), XVIII (1935), 267–331.

13. Rowland and Sanders, *Mississippi Provincial Archives*, II, 344, 377, 430.

14. *Ibid.*, 627.

15. *Ibid.*, 494.

16. *Ibid.*, 655.

17. *Ibid.*, 603. In November, 1728, the authorities in Louisiana reported to France that two masons sent from Europe had arrived. "Now we have no building done except in bricks."

18. Rowland and Sanders, *Mississippi Provincial Archives*, V (Baton Rouge, 1984), 116.

19. Wilson, *Colonial Louisiana*, 245–246.

20. Samuel Wilson, Jr., "Colonial Fortifications and Military Architecture" in John Francis McDermott, ed., *The French in the Mississippi Valley* (Urbana, 1965), 110.

21. Edwin Adams Davis, *Louisiana, A Narrative History* (Baton Rouge, 1971), 60.

22. Gravier and Blanchard, "Voyage of the Ursuline Nuns," 81.

23. Rowland and Sanders, *Mississippi Provincial Archives*, II, 557–558.

24. Philip Pittman, *The Present State of the European Settlements on the Mississippi* (London, 1770), 42–43.

25. Records and Deliberations of the Cabildo, IV, typescript, WPA, 1936.

26. "New Orleans, 1801: An Account by John Pintard," *LHQ*, XXXIV (1951), 226.

27. "The Journal of Dr. John Sibley," *LHQ*, X (1927), 486–487.

28. Christian Schultz, *Travels on an Inland Voyage* (New York, 1810), II, 190.

29. "The Journal of Dr. John Sibley," *LHQ*, X (1927), 482.

30. Harriet P. Bos, "Barthélémy Lafon," M.A. thesis, Tulane University, 1977.

31. "New Orleans, 1801: An Account by John Pintard," *LHQ*, XXXIV (1951), 226.

32. "The Journal of Dr. John Sibley," 486.

II. THE FEDERAL ERA

1. Paul F. Lachance, "The 1809 Immigration of Saint-Dominique Refugees to New Orleans," *Louisiana History*, XXIX (1988), 109–141.

2. Peter M. Wolf, "Jean Hyacinthe Laclotte," M.A. thesis, Tulane University, 1963.

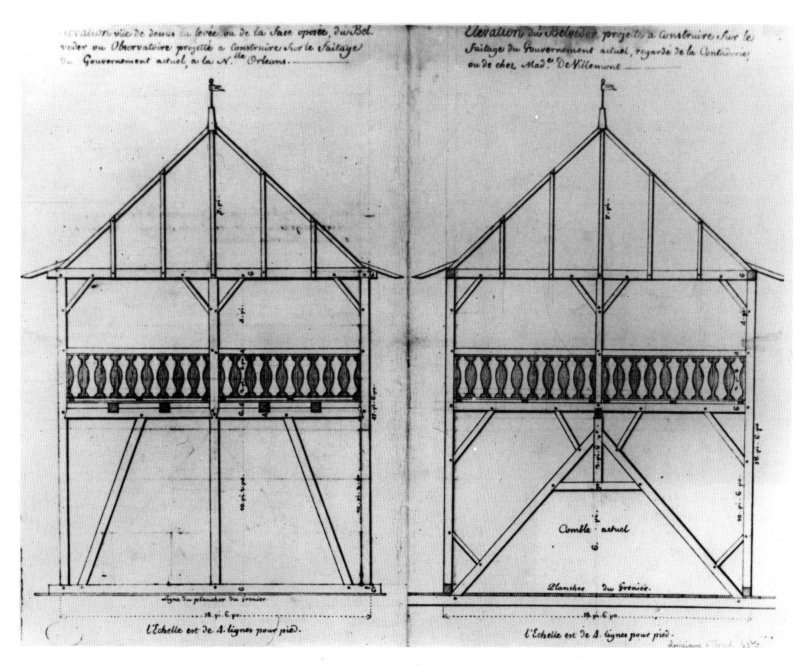

Drawing of unidentified French colonial building "near the levee opposite the tower of the proposed observatory." *Historic New Orleans Collection*

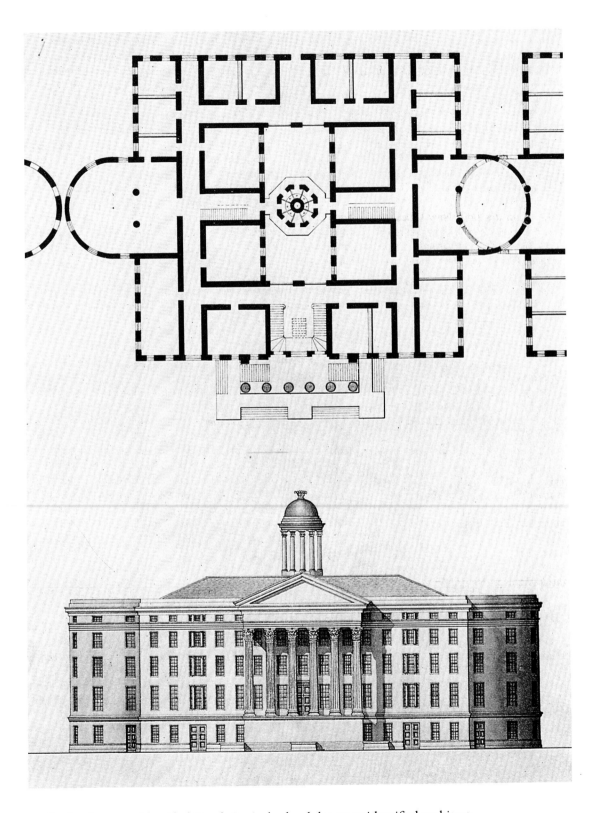

Design for an unidentified Greek Revival school, by an unidentified architect, c. 1845. *Southeastern Architectural Archive, Tulane University Library*

3. Quoted in biographical file on Laclotte at Historic New Orleans Collection, New Orleans. The author is indebted to this and other biographical files at HNOC for information about architects and builders in New Orleans.

4. "Project of a Play-House for the Town of New Orleans," broadside, 1805, Historic New Orleans Collection.

5. *Moniteur*, New Orleans, February 28, 1807.

6. *Courier*, New Orleans, October 8, 1810.

7. *Louisiana Gazette*, New Orleans, September 28, 1810.

8. *L'Ami des Lois*, New Orleans, July 27, 1813.

9. *Courier*, New Orleans, March 18, 1808.

10. In the *Courier*, August 27, 1810, Pilié announced that he had been associated with Lafon for "several years."

11. Joseph Holt Ingraham, *South-West by a Yankee* (New York, 1835).

12. *The Bee*, New Orleans, December 20, 1827.

13. The author is indebted to Ann M. Masson for sharing with him her research on dePouilly.

14. The Improvement Company of New Orleans offered $500 for the best plan submitted for the St. Louis Exchange Hotel. *Louisiana Courier*, New Orleans, June 24, 1835; *The Bee*, New Orleans, June 1, 1835.

15. *The Bee*, New Orleans, November 25, 1837.

16. *Gibson's Guide and Directory of Louisiana and the Cities of New Orleans and Lafayette* (New Orleans, 1838), 330.

17. DePouilly's drawings are filed with building contract, dated August 22, 1836, Theodore Seghers, notary, Vol. 18, No. 277, Notarial Archives, New Orleans.

18. Building contract for Marianne Olivier, April 8, 1839, L. T. Claire, notary, Vol. 71, No. 251, Notarial Archives, New Orleans.

19. Building contracts: (Poydras Street Theater) August 25, 1842, F. Grima, notary, Vol. 37, No. 258; (St. Augustine Church) June 20, 1842, L. T. Claire, notary, Vol. 86, No. 364; (Bertus House) March 17, 1842, A. Ducatel, notary, Vol. 18, No. 57; (Avart House) July 14, 1842, Felix Grima, notary, Vol. 37, No. 232; (dePaula Para House) November 7, 1846, E. Barnett, notary, Vol. 34, No. 362; (Graihle Store) August 2, 1849, T. Guyal, notary, Vol. 13, No. 474; (Trudeau Stores) June 25, 1849, T. Guyal, notary, Vol. 13, No. 402, Notarial Archives, New Orleans.

20. Building contracts, March 12, 1849, J. Cuvillier, notary, Vol. 52, No. 52; June 25, 1849, A. Chiapella, notary, Vol. 17, No. 324, Notarial Archives, New Orleans.

21. "Description of the Plan of the Custom House to be erected at New Orleans, and the manner of constructing the same," in John C. Van Horne, *The Correspondence and Miscellaneous Papers of Benjamin Henry Latrobe*, II (New Haven, 1986), 413–421.

22. John C. Van Horne, *The Correspondence and Miscellaneous Papers of . . . Latrobe*, III (New Haven, 1988), 138.

23. Wilson, *The Vieux Carré*, 110.

24. Van Horne, *Correspondence and Miscellaneous Papers of . . . Latrobe*, III, 1028.

25. "Instructions for building the Banking House of the State Bank of Louisiana," August 10, 1820, in Louisiana State Bank Papers, Louisiana State University, Baton Rouge.

26. Benjamin Latrobe to Robert Goodloe Harper, August 27, 1820, in Van Horne, *Op. cit.*, III, 1061.

27. Edward C. Carter II, *et al.*, *The Journals of Benjamin Henry Latrobe*, III (New Haven, 1980), 185, 194, 267.

28. *Ibid.*, 194–195.

29. A. Oakley Hall, *The Manhattaner in New Orleans* (New York, 1851), 35.

30. Interior of the Camp Street Theater is described in *Courier*, New Orleans, December 19, 1828.

31. *The Bee*, New Orleans, April 7, 1835, and September 18, 1835.

32. *Daily Picayune*, New Orleans, November 6, 1840.

33. *Courier*, New Orleans, October 29, 1821.

34. *Louisiana Gazette*, New Orleans, January 7, 1824; *Courier*, New Orleans, May 15, 1830; *Louisiana Advertiser*, New Orleans, June 20, 1826.

35. *The Bee*, New Orleans, October 24, 1834.

36. *Daily Delta*, New Orleans, September 23, 1851.

37. Building contract, June 25, 1835, W. Y. Lewis, notary, Vol. 20, Notarial Archives, New Orleans.

III. THE LOUISIANA PLANTATION HOUSE

1. Wilson, *Colonial Louisiana*, 267–272.

2. Carolyn M. Wells, "Architecture of Colonial Natchitoches," Northwestern State University, 1973.

3. See Jay Edwards, *Louisiana's French Vernacular Architecture: A Historical and Social Bibliography* (Monticello, Indiana, 1986), and Jonathan Fricker, "The Origins of the Creole Raised Plantation House," *Louisiana History*, XXV (1984), 137–155.

4. R. Christopher Goodwin, *et al.*, *Elmwood: The Historical Archaeology of a Southeastern Louisiana Plantation* (Metarie, 1984).

5. Wilson, *Colonial Louisiana*, 378–381.

6. Charles Robin, *A Voyage to Louisiana* (New Orleans, 1966), 122.

7. "Southern Louisiana and Southern Alabama in 1819: The Journal of James Leander Cathcart," *LHQ*, XXVIII (1945), 93–94.

「I92」

8. The author is indebted to the indefatigable Robert S. Brantley for information about construction of Madame Bertrand's house.

9. Powell A. Casey, *Encyclopedia of Forts, Posts, Named Camps and Other Military Installations in Louisiana* (Baton Rouge, 1983), 14–16, 84–92.

10. Laura Adams Wooldridge, "The East Feliciana Parish Courthouse and Lawyers' Row in Clinton, Louisiana," M.A. thesis, Tulane University, c. 1972.

11. The author is indebted to Patricia Kahle, Assistant Director, The Shadows-on-the-Teche, for copies of the letters quoted in this paragraph.

12. Samuel Wilson, Jr., "Evergreen Plantation," typescript, 1987. The author is grateful to Mr. Wilson for sharing this unpublished research paper.

13. Goodloe R. Stuck, "Log Houses in Northwest Louisiana," *Louisiana Studies*, X (1971), 225–237. The author is indebted to Mr. Stuck for an afternoon's touring in northern Louisiana and for generous help.

14. Mary Marshall to Henry Marshall, January 9, 1844, Marshall-Furman Collection, Hill Memorial Library, Louisiana State University, Baton Rouge. The author is indebted to Francis Chandler Furman, Knoxville, Tennessee, for permission to quote from this letter.

15. Frederick Law Olmsted, *The Cotton Kingdom* (New York, 1966), 280.

16. Ola Mae Wood, *Reflections of Rosedown* (St. Francisville, Louisiana, n.d.), 16.

17. Jacob E. Pulwers, "Henry Marston," M.A. thesis, Louisiana State University, 1955.

18. Charles L. Dufour, "Henry Howard, Forgotten Architect," *Journal of the Society of Architectural Historians*, II (1952), 21. See also "Henry Howard, Architect," exhibition catalogue, Louisiana Landmarks Society, 1952.

19. Albert Diettel, Notebook, Louisiana State University Library, Baton Rouge.

20. Building contract, June 8, 1857, in "John Hampden Randolph, a Southern Planter," M.A. thesis, Louisiana State University, 1936.

21. Henry Howard to John H. Randolph, August 19, 1859, Randolph Papers, Louisiana State University, Baton Rouge.

IV. THE GREEK REVIVAL

1. Timothy Flint, *History and Geography of the Mississippi Valley* (Cincinnati, 1833), I, 267.

2. Edward C. Carter II, *et al.*, *The Journals of Benjamin Henry Latrobe*, III (New Haven, 1980), 267.

3. Building contract, 1831, J. Cuvillier, notary, Vol. 1, No. 119, Notarial Archives, New Orleans.

4. Charles J. Collins, "A History of the U.S. Mint, New Orleans, Louisiana," typescript, 1970.

5. Strickland's drawings are attached to the building contract, 1835, J. Cuvillier, notary, Vol. 6, No. 19, Notarial Archives, New Orleans.

6. James Gallier, *Autobiography of James Gallier, Architect* (Paris, 1864), 9; see also Samuel E. Wilson, Jr., "James Gallier, Architect," exhibition catalogue, typescript, 1950.

7. Gallier, *Autobiography*, 19.

8. *Ibid.*, 20.

9. *Ibid.*, 21.

10. *Gibson's Guide and Directory of Louisiana and the Cities of New Orleans and Lafayette* (New Orleans, 1838), 318.

11. *Picayune*, New Orleans, April 16, 1837, reported that the Church was "very nearly completed."

12. *Courier*, New Orleans, September 3, 1836.

13. *The Bee*, New Orleans, April 21, 1835, April 24, 1835, May 4, 1835.

14. The connection between the Tremont House and the St. Charles Hotel is explored in James Robert Bienvenu, "Two Greek Revival Hotels in New Orleans," M.A. thesis, Tulane University, 1961.

15. *The Bee*, New Orleans, May 13, 1835.

16. Gallier, *Autobiography*, 22.

17. The St. Charles is described in detail in James S. Buckingham, *The Slave States of America* (London, 1842), 331–332, and also in *Gibson's Guide*, 332–333.

18. *Daily Picayune*, New Orleans, January 16, 1851.

19. *Daily Picayune*, February 14, 1851, and August 4, 1852.

20. The Odd Fellows Hall is described in *Daily Courier*, New Orleans, August 18, 1849, and *Daily Picayune*, New Orleans, October 12, 1852.

21. The erection of the steeple of the Presbyterian Church was a spectacular event. The steeple was prefabricated within the walls of its tower, then raised into place with the aid of pulleys and ropes. The Church was wrecked in a 1915 hurricane, rebuilt, and finally demolished in 1938.

22. The second St. Charles Hotel was described in the *Daily Picayune*, New Orleans, January 11, 1853.

23. Building contract, November 21, 1835, H. B. Cenas, notary, Vol. 5, No. 173, Notarial Archives, New Orleans.

24. Building contracts: (Samuel Moore) January 28, 1836, H. B. Cenas, notary, Vol. 6, No. 253; (Antoine Jonau) July 13, 1836, L. T. Claire, notary, Vol. 52, No. 636, Notarial Archives, New Orleans.

25. Building contract, October 27, 1836, H. B. Cenas, notary, Vol. 10, No. 221, Notarial Archives, New Orleans.

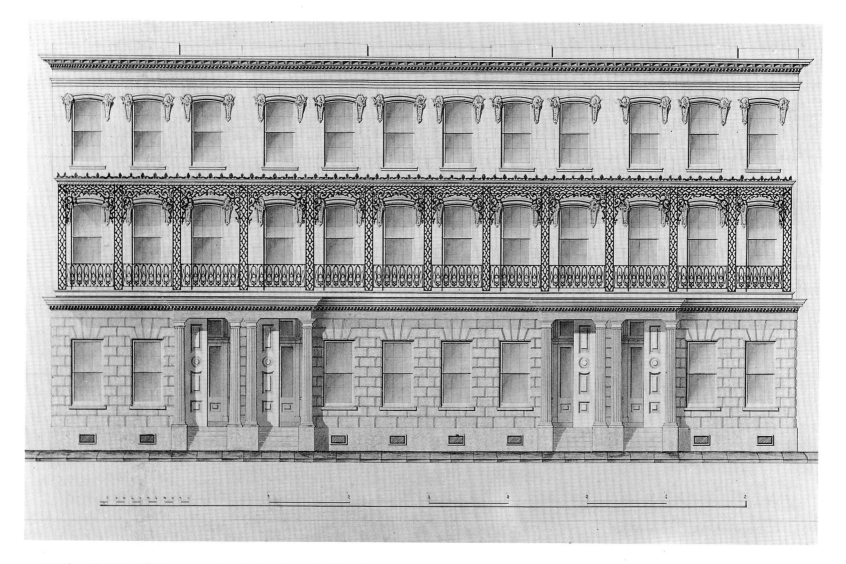

Unidentified block of houses, elevation by James Gallier, Jr., c. 1855. *Historic New Orleans Collection*

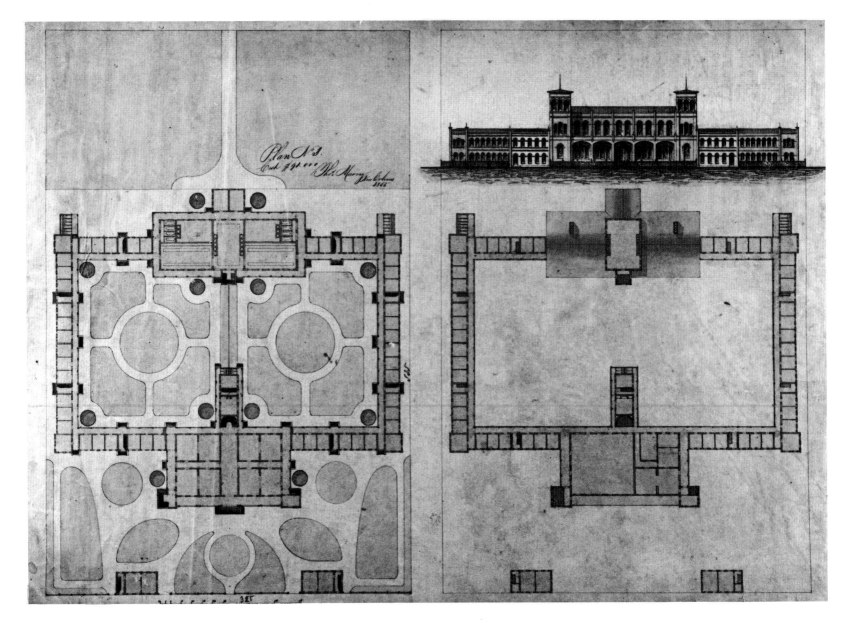

Design for an unidentified Italianate hospital, perhaps the second Marine Hospital at New Orleans, by Thomas Murray, 1855. *Southeastern Architectural Archive, Tulane University Library*

26. Building contract, April 23, 1838, D. L. McCay, notary, Vol. 5, Nos. 49 and 64, Notarial Archives, New Orleans.

27. Building contract, June 15, 1838, F. Grima, notary, Vol. 21, No. 362, Notarial Archives, New Orleans.

28. "Estimate of a house for Doctor Mercer in Canal Street," April 15, 1844, in Gallier Notebook, Labrot Collection, Southeastern Architectural Archive, Tulane University, New Orleans. The building contract, May 21, 1844, H. B. Cenas, notary, Vol. 31, No. 789, Notarial Archives, New Orleans.

29. *Daily Delta*, New Orleans, February 20, 1848.

30. The capstone of the portico was raised into place, *Daily Picayune*, New Orleans, February 21, 1851.

31. "Estimate for the Commercial Exchange, St. Charles Street," in Gallier Notebook, Tulane University.

32. Gallier, *Autobiography*, 41.

33. Leonard V. Huber and Samuel Wilson, Jr., *Baroness Pontalba's Buildings* (New Orleans, 1964).

34. *Courier*, New Orleans, February 7, 1837.

35. *Gibson's Guide*, 321.

36. *Lafayette City Advertiser*, November 12, 1842, quoted in Arthur Scully, Jr., *James Dakin, Architect* (Baton Rouge, 1973), a marvelous, pioneering survey of Dakin's career, to which the author is much indebted.

37. Stanley C. Arthur, "A History of the U.S. Custom House, New Orleans," typescript, W.P.A., 1940, revised by Samuel Wilson, Jr. (Washington, 1982).

38. Dakin diary, 26, Dakin Collection, Louisiana State University Library, Baton Rouge.

39. *Louisiana Courier*, New Orleans, July 28, 1835.

40. Dakin diary, 41, Dakin Collection, Louisiana State University Library.

41. *Daily Picayune*, New Orleans, January 4, 1843.

42. Thomas K. Wharton, diary, 1854, 303–304, New York Public Library.

43. *Ibid.*, 343.

V. ROMANTIC STYLES

1. Edward C. Carter, II., *The Journals of Benjamin Henry Latrobe*, III (New Haven, 1980), 226.

2. R. R. Gurley, *Life and Eloquence of the Rev. Sylvester Larned* (New York, 1844), 61.

3. *Ibid.*, 61.

4. *Ibid.*, 67.

5. *Daily Picayune*, New Orleans, July 3, 1838.

6. "I had to take out the old foundation and put in a new one, without pulling down the walls. . . . The whole of the interior arrangements, the groined ceilings, the altar, the organ, &c., were erected after my designs." James Gallier, *Autobiography of James Gallier, Architect* (Paris, 1864), 28.

7. William Eugene Rooney, "The New Orleans Marine Hospital, 1802–1861," M.A. thesis, Tulane University, 1950. The author is also indebted to information from Pamela Scott, Associate Editor, Robert Mills Papers, Smithsonian Institution.

8. Proposal for Marine Hospital, September 1, 1837, with letter from Mills to James Breedlove, September 1, 1837, in Mills Papers, Southeastern Architectural Archives, Tulane University, New Orleans.

9. Thomas K. Wharton, diary, 1832, 235, New York Public Library.

10. Wharton diary, 1854, 386, New York Public Library.

11. *Ibid.*, 386.

12. Wharton diary, 1854, 280; 1855–56, 45, 188, 218–219, 243; 1857, 8, 62, New York Public Library.

13. The author is indebted to Leon LeSueur of Napoleonville and G. K. Pratt Munson of New Iberia for information about Christ Church and copies from the vestry minutes of April, 1854.

14. James Dakin letter, January 26, 1847, in Dakin, diary, Louisiana State University Library.

15. Maunsell White to James Dakin, May 31, 1848, White Papers, Louisiana State University Library.

16. Dakin diary, 86–87, Louisiana State University Library.

17. *Ibid.*, 121.

18. *Daily Delta*, New Orleans, February 13, 1852.

19. *Daily Crescent*, New Orleans, April 25, 1853; building contract, March 2, 1853, H. B. Cenas, notary, Vol. 55, No. 625, Notarial Archives, New Orleans.

20. Building contract, May 18, 1854, Richard Brenan, notary, Notarial Archives, New Orleans.

21. William R. Cullison, III, "Orange Grove, the Design and Construction of an Ante-bellum Neo-Gothic Plantation House on the Mississippi River," M.A. thesis, Tulane University, 1969.

22. Sandra L. Tatman and Roger W. Moss, *Biographical Dictionary of Philadelphia Architects* (Philadelphia, 1985), 422–423.

23. Maunsell White to James Dakin, January 27, 1849, White Papers, Louisiana State University Library.

24. William Barrow Floyd, *The Barrow Family of Old Louisiana* (Lexington, Kentucky, 1963), 30.

25. These two villas are illustrated in Georgia Payne Durham Pinkston, *A Place to Remember* (Baton Rouge, 1977).

26. *Daily Picayune*, New Orleans, April 1, 1857.

27. *Daily Picayune,* New Orleans, January 20, 1855.

28. "Estimate for M. Heine's Dwellings," in Gallier Notebook, Labrot Collection, Southeastern Architectural Archives, Tulane University.

29. Thomas K. Wharton, diary, September 24, 1859, New York Public Library.

30. *New Orleans Delta,* May 23, 1859; *Daily Picayune,* New Orleans, December 3, 1859.

31. *Daily Picayune,* New Orleans, July 14, 1857.

32. *Daily Picayune,* New Orleans, August 3, 1852.

33. *Building contract,* February 10, 1859, A. Mazareau, notary, Vol. 53, No. 90, Notarial Archives, New Orleans.

34. Thomas K. Wharton, diary, 1854, 429, New York Public Library.

Index